TOKYO
Travel guide 2024

Richard Caraway

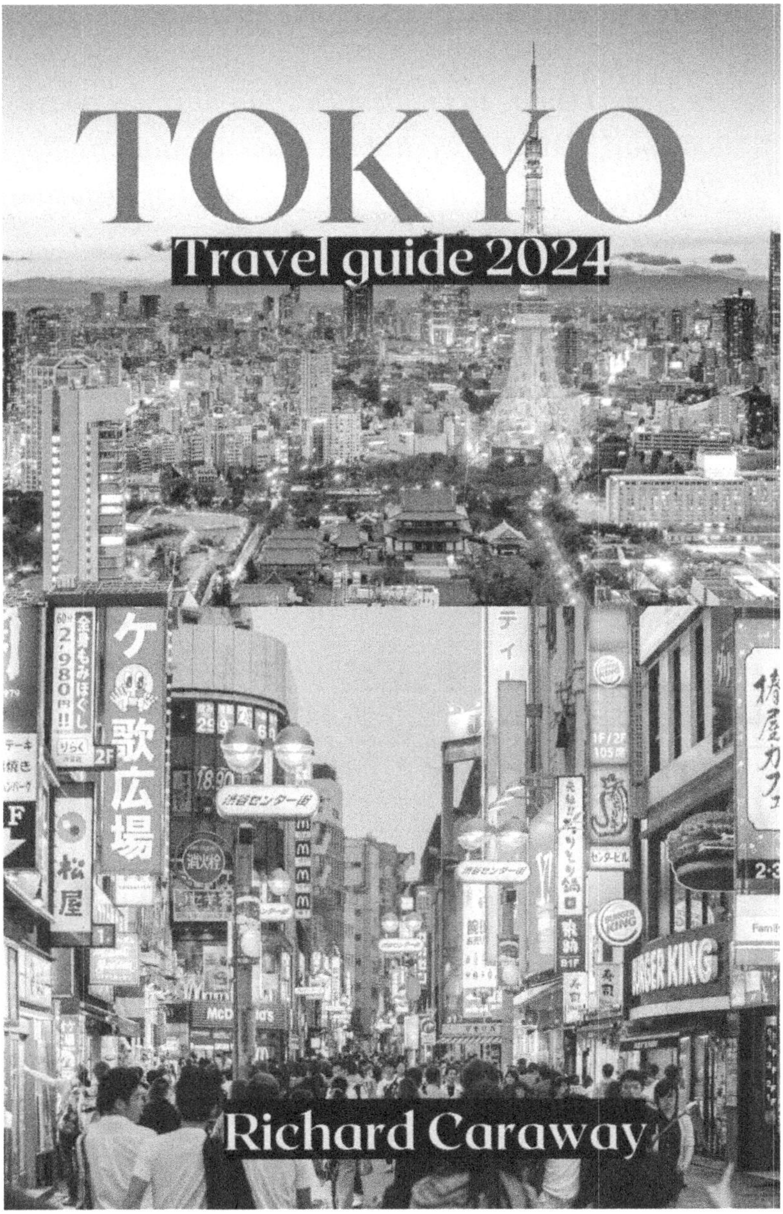

Tokyo Travel Guide 2024

An Expert Guide to the Best Destinations, Japanese Food, Culture, Night Life, Accommodations, Shopping, Money Saving Tips With A lot of Pictures, 5-Day Itinerary and Maps

Richard Caraway

Copyright © 2023 Richard Caraway. All rights reserved.

No part of this guidebook may be reproduced, stored in a retrieval system, or transmitted in any form or by any means, electronic, mechanical, photocopying, recording, or otherwise, without the prior written permission of the copyright holder, except for brief quotations embodied in critical reviews and certain other noncommercial uses permitted by copyright law.

This comprehensive travel guidebook is a labor of love and dedication, designed to inspire and assist travelers in their quest for unforgettable adventures. Packed with valuable insights, expert recommendations, and captivating narratives, it is the result of extensive research and personal exploration by the author.

Table of Contents

INTRODUCTION 8
CHAPTER 1 13
INTRODUCTION TO TOKYO 13
   WELCOME TO TOKYO 13
   A BRIEF HISTORY OF TOKYO 18
   TOKYO'S UNIQUE CULTURE 22
   25 INTERESTING FACTS ABOUT TOKYO 28
CHAPTER 2 35
PLANNING YOUR TRIP 35
   WHEN TO VISIT TOKYO 35
   BUDGETING FOR YOUR TRIP 37
   TRAVELING TIPS TO TOKYO 40
   WHERE TO EXCHANGE CURRENCY 44
   JAPAN VISA 46
   MONEY-SAVING TIPS FOR TRAVELERS IN TOKYO
   47
CHAPTER 3 51
GETTING AROUND TOKYO 51
   NAVIGATING TOKYO'S TRANSPORTATION 51
   TOKYO METRO AND JR PASS 55
   BIKING AND WALKING IN TOKYO 57
   TRAVELLING TO TOKYO AND GETTING AROUND.
   60
CHAPTER 4 65

TOKYO'S NEIGHBORHOODS AND TOP DESTINATIONS 65
   SHINJUKU: THE HEART OF TOKYO 65
   SHIBUYA: TOKYO'S TRENDSETTING DISTRICT... 70
   ASAKUSA: TRADITION MEETS MODERNITY 74
   AKIHABARA: Tokyo's Electrifying Nerve Center 78
   GINZA 82
CHAPTER 5 87
TOP ATTRACTIONS IN TOKYO YOU SHOULD VISIT.... 87
   TOKYO DISNEYLAND AND DISNEYSEA 87
   SENSO-JI TEMPLE AND ASAKUSA CULTURE 92
   TSUKIJI FISH MARKET AND CULINARY DELIGHTS 95
   KOISHIKAWA KORAKUEN: A Timeless Oasis 98
   TEAMLAB PLANETS: An Immersive Digital Wonderland 100
CHAPTER 6 102
DINING AND CUISINE 102
   SUSHI AND SASHIMI 102
   RAMEN, TEMPURA, AND OTHER JAPANESE DELICACIES 105
   IZAKAYAS AND JAPANESE DINING ETIQUETTE 110
CHAPTER 7 114
SHOPPING IN TOKYO 114
   AKIHABARA: ELECTRONICS AND ANIME 114
   HARAJUKU: FASHION AND STREETWEAR 118
   TRADITIONAL CRAFTS AND SOUVENIRS 122

CHAPTER 8 128

TOKYO'S NIGHTLIFE 128

    KARAOKE AND ENTERTAINMENT 128

    NIGHTCLUBS AND BARS 132

    NIGHTTIME VIEWS OF TOKYO 136

CHAPTER 9 142

DAY TRIPS FROM TOKYO 142

    BEST DAY TRIPS 142

    NIKKO: TEMPLES AND NATURAL BEAUTY 146

    KAMAKURA: HISTORY AND BEACHES 147

    HAKONE: HOT SPRINGS AND SCENIC BEAUTY .. 147

CHAPTER 10 149

WHERE TO SLEEP AND OTHER PRACTICAL INFORMATION 149

    ACCOMMODATION OPTIONS 149

    SAFETY AND HEALTH TIPS 157

    ESSENTIAL JAPANESE WORDS AND PHRASES FOR TOURISTS 160

CHAPTER 11 166

TOKYO 5 DAY ITINERARY 166

    DAY 1: EXPLORE THE HEART OF TOKYO 166

    DAY 2: SHIBUYA AND SURROUNDING GEMS 171

    DAY 3: TOKYO'S HISTORIC AND MODERN BLEND 175

    DAY 4: TOKYO'S URBAN DIVERSITY AND CULINARY DELIGHTS 177

**DAY 5: TOKYO'S CULTURAL HERITAGE AND
HIDDEN GEMS** 181

INTRODUCTION

Let me guess, maybe you are a person who wants to visit Tokyo for the first time and now you want to equip yourself with more knowledge? Let me assure you have the right resource and that is this book. It takes care of all types of visitors to Tokyo from family visits, company tours, lonely visitors, first time visitors and even the explorers who just want to explore what this magical mega city has to offer. By the way, I am Richard Caraway and thank you for choosing this Tokyo master guide. In this book I have ensured that I have given the best suggestions ever on the best destinations, where exactly to go, when to go there, what to do, what to see, what to eat, what not to forget taking photos and everything else you will want to know.

With the best destination for many years, Tokyo—the city that never sleeps—has been a part of my life. I've gotten to know its lively culture better with each visit, hunted out its hidden treasures, and appreciated its culinary treats. I can't help but think back on the innumerable memories Tokyo has left indelible in my heart as I stand on the threshold of this trip—a journey of sharing my experiences with you.

Tokyo has always captivated me, even before I set foot on its busy streets. Growing up in the United States, I was drawn to the mystique of Japan—the land of the rising sun. I was captivated by the appeal of the coexistence of antiquated customs and cutting-edge technology, the contrast between quiet temples and neon-lit neighborhoods, and the prospect of culinary explorations.

I started an academic journey in my quest for knowledge by enrolling at the Kyoto Institute of Technology for my master's degree. I had no idea that my choice would initiate a long-lasting love affair with Japan. While Kyoto served as my location of study, Tokyo served as my playground, where every weekend offered the promise of discovering something new.

The Tokyo Diaries

During my first trips to Tokyo, I was eager to explore new places. Every alleyway and every turn had a surprise for a novice. I walked around neighborhoods like Shinjuku, the hub of the city's vibrant nightlife, and Akihabara, where technology and pop culture merge.

But it was my second trip, during which I lived in Tokyo for seven years, that made me a true Tokyoite. I spent that time navigating the confusing streets, interacting with the residents, and learning about the best-kept secrets of the city. Tokyo shaped my life, from enjoying the cherry blossoms at Ueno Park to devouring sushi in Tsukiji Market.

Learning Japanese in Tokyo

Language, they say, is the key to a culture's heart. Understanding this, I dedicated two years to immerse myself in the Japanese language. I aimed to communicate like a true Japanese, not simply touch the surface. I've engaged in innumerable conversations with store owners, cab drivers, and other tourists that have transformed me from a visitor into a participant in the colorful tapestry of the city.

I now consider myself to be fluent and speak the language like a real Japanese. This fluency has enriched my Tokyo odyssey beyond measure by opening doors to hidden experiences and deeper connections.

A Tokyo Travel Guide Born from Experience

This travel guide is a labor of love, born from my countless adventures in Tokyo. I've personally tried every itinerary, savored every culinary delight, and rested my head in the suggested accommodations. Each suggestion on these pages has been carefully chosen and imbued with first-hand knowledge to provide you the most authentic and unforgettable trip to Tokyo.

Tokyo's Hidden Treasures Unlocked

Tokyo is a hidden gem full of adventures just waiting to be discovered. This guide will take you on a quick tour of Tokyo's various neighborhoods, taking you from the quiet temples of Asakusa to the stylish streets of Harajuku, from the serene gardens of Koishikawa Korakuen to the electric energy of Akihabara.

Tokyo has something to offer everyone, whether you're a die-hard eater looking for the ideal bowl of ramen, an art enthusiast looking for digital wonders at teamLab Borderless, or a history buff exploring the depths of Meiji Jingu Shrine. With this guide, I hope to empower you to embrace Tokyo's unique blend of tradition and modernity.

So, fellow travelers, as you embark on your Tokyo adventure, know that you're not alone. I'm here with you, sharing the wisdom and stories Tokyo has bestowed upon me. I dare you to try what I have tried and you will create memories that will last in your lifetime. Wish you a safe travel, best experience and an enjoyable voyage. Much Love!!!

CHAPTER 1

INTRODUCTION TO TOKYO

WELCOME TO TOKYO

Hey there, fellow traveler! Welcome to Tokyo (東京, Tōkyō), Japan's vibrant capital and arguably the most mesmerizing metropolis in the world. I'm excited to be your virtual tour guide as we embark on this adventure through the beating heart of Japan. Tokyo is a sprawling city of contrasts, where ancient traditions and cutting-edge technology harmoniously coexist. So, let's dive in and discover this incredible city together.

Tokyo: A Brief Introduction

Let me quickly recap Tokyo's remarkable qualities before we dig further into this buzzing urban wonderland. Tokyo is not just any city; it is a vibrant combination of tradition, modernity, and history. It is a vast megalopolis made up of 23 major city wards and a collection of outlying cities, towns, and villages that is nestled within Japan's largest prefecture. And don't forget about the nearby islands of Izu and Ogasawara, which are likewise governed by Tokyo and provide a taste of heaven.

A Glimpse into Tokyo's Past

To truly appreciate Tokyo, we need to rewind the clock a bit. This bustling city was known as Edo before 1868. It was a small castle town back then, tucked up beneath Mount Fuji. But when Tokugawa Ieyasu, a great character in Japanese history, chose to set up his feudal administration here in 1603, everything changed. Edo prospered and expanded, becoming one of the biggest cities in the world.

https://www.google.com/maps/d/u/0/edit?mid=1z60QUaHLd6Jqx6LbWRThNxnG07EsoZM&ll=36.02793769283987%2C138.1273560453125&z=8

Then, the pivotal moment arrived with the Meiji Restoration of 1868. Kyoto became the new home of the emperor and

15

the political heart of Japan, while Edo was swiftly renamed Tokyo, which means "Eastern Capital." Tokyo had a quick change, becoming the focal point of Japan's modernization.

But Tokyo's journey wasn't without its difficulties. Large portions of the city were destroyed in 1923 by the Great Kanto Earthquake, which also left a path of devastation in its wake. And if that weren't enough, the city suffered greatly from World War II air raids in 1945. Tokyo, however, persevered and emerged from the ruins stronger and more lively than ever.

The Tokyo of Today

Fast forward to the present day, and you'll find a Tokyo that is nothing short of extraordinary. It's a city that offers an endless array of experiences to its visitors. Whether you're a history buff, a shopaholic, a foodie, or an art enthusiast, Tokyo has something special just for you.

Starting with the historical period. Tokyo blatantly shows its past, and areas like Asakusa transport you back in time. You can wander down Nakamise-dori and take in the atmosphere while discovering old temples. Don't forget to visit Senso-ji Temple in Tokyo, the city's oldest temple and a symbol of the region's rich spiritual legacy.

Tokyo, however, is not just about the past; it constantly pushes the limits of innovation and technology. This is demonstrated by the neon-lit Shinjuku districts and the busy Shibuya Crossing. In Akihabara, you may explore a futuristic world of electronics and anime, and in Harajuku, you can see Tokyo's cutting-edge fashion industry.

Now let's discuss the food, which is one of my personal favorites. Tokyo is a cuisine lover's paradise. Your taste buds are in for a treat with everything from famous sushi and sashimi to tasty bowls of ramen and crunchy tempura. Don't forget to take a stroll around the beautiful Golden Gai lanes for a taste of Tokyo's charming bar culture.

Despite having the appearance of being a concrete jungle, there are peaceful green spaces in Tokyo. Beautiful green areas like Shinjuku Gyoen and Ueno Park provide a calm haven from the hustle and bustle of the metropolis. These open spaces offer a chance to relax, take a picnic, or perhaps admire the cherry blossoms' springtime splendor.

Get Ready for an Unforgettable Journey

So, fellow explorer, are you prepared to set off on this extraordinary tour through Tokyo? You will fall in love with the captivating blend of tradition and modernity that distinguishes this amazing metropolis as we delve further into the city's neighborhoods, attractions, eating, and so much more. Tokyo is more than simply a place to go; it's an experience, a feeling, and a whole world just waiting to be discovered. Let's make every moment count in this remarkable city that never sleeps.

A BRIEF HISTORY OF TOKYO

Picture Tokyo today, with its glittering skyscrapers, bustling streets, and vibrant culture, and it's easy to forget that this city has a history spanning centuries. Tokyo's evolution is a captivating tale of political intrigue, natural disasters, resilience, and unrelenting progress.

The Early Years: Edo

Our journey starts in the modest castle town of Edo. Edo, which is located on the eastern coast of Japan's Honshu Island, was not the bustling city we know it to be today. When Tokugawa Ieyasu, a powerful feudal lord, chose Edo as the capital of his shogunate—the Tokugawa Shogunate—early in the 17th century, Edo rose to prominence. The strategic location and closeness to the sea made Edo the perfect site for a center of political power.

Edo grew under Tokugawa administration. The city quickly expanded from a tiny fishing community to one of the biggest in the world, with a population that surpassed major European towns like London and Paris. The shogunate gave stability to Japan, resulting in the Edo period (1603–1868), a protracted period of calm. During this time, Edo flourished as a center of invention, trade, and culture.

The Meiji Restoration: Tokyo is Born

With the Meiji Restoration in 1868, Japan experienced a period of transformation. As the shogunate lost its political sway and the emperor reclaimed it, Japan started its modernisation process. To represent this change, the emperor and his administration moved from Kyoto to Edo, which was soon renamed Tokyo, which means "Eastern Capital."

Tokyo underwent a quick and complete transformation. Urban planning and infrastructural improvements influenced by Western designs. Modern buildings, railroads, and expansive boulevards started to shape the cityscape.

Challenges and Resilience: Natural Disasters and War

Tokyo's path to greatness was not without its challenges. In 1923, a catastrophic event struck—the Great Kanto Earthquake. This devastating quake and the subsequent fires left large parts of the city in ruins. But the people of Tokyo showed wonderful resilience. They reconstructed their city with tenacity, creating an even more advanced and durable Tokyo.

It wasn't the end of the challenges. Tokyo was the target of air strikes during World War II, which caused significant damage. After the war, the city's revival was nothing short of amazing. It was evidence of the residents' unbreakable spirit as they transformed Tokyo into a city that would eventually dazzle the globe.

Tokyo Today: A Global Megacity

Fast forward to the present, and Tokyo is a global megacity, a pulsating hub of culture, commerce, and technology. It is a place where cutting-edge innovation coexists peacefully with age-old traditions. Tokyo's diverse personality includes the neon signs of Shinjuku, the well-known Shibuya Crossing, and the calm temples of Asakusa.

The city is still developing and pushing the limits of what is possible. It's a city where skyscrapers reach the sky, where bullet trains take you across the nation in a flash, and where global audiences are captivated by pop cultural phenomenon like anime and manga.

TOKYO'S UNIQUE CULTURE

Tokyo isn't just a city; it's a living canvas of diverse cultural influences, and every step you take reveals something new and intriguing. From ancient customs to contemporary art, Tokyo's culture is a rich tapestry waiting to be unraveled.

1. Traditional Arts and Crafts

You might notice Tokyo's intense appreciation for its traditional arts and crafts as one of the first things. In the city, you can see how long-standing customs continue to exist. Discover the realm of kimono artistry in Asakusa, where skilled craftspeople painstakingly make these priceless garments. Don't pass up the opportunity to witness experienced artisans at work in places like Nihonbashi, where you can observe the art of sword making, known as "tsuba."

Image showing Kimono traditional garmet

2. Tea Ceremony: A Soothing Ritual

The "chanoyu," or Japanese tea ceremony, is a contemplative and heavily ritualized activity. You have the chance to take part in this peaceful ritual in Tokyo. Matcha tea may be enjoyed while being surrounded by lush gardens at old tea houses like Happo-en, where you can fully experience Japanese aesthetics.

3. Festivals All Year Round

Tokyo loves to celebrate, and there's a festival for every season. The cherry blossom festivals in spring, known as "hanami," are a breathtaking sight. Streets are adorned with lanterns during Tanabata, the Star Festival. In August, join the spirited Bon Odori dance festivals to honor ancestors. And the list goes on; there's always a reason to join the festivities.

4. Modern Art and Pop Culture

Pop culture and modern art are both centered in Tokyo. In Roppongi, the Mori Art Museum exhibits contemporary Japanese and foreign artwork. Visit artistic hotspots like Koenji and Nakano, noted for their burgeoning indie and street art movements, for a deeper look at Tokyo's creative landscape.

The global phenomenon of anime and manga is another. The Akihabara neighborhood of Tokyo, sometimes known as "Electric Town," is a haven for devotees of these genres of art. Discover the themed restaurants, cafes, and shops that are devoted to your favorite characters.

5. Harajuku: Where Fashion Knows No Bounds

Harajuku, Tokyo's epicenter of fashion and youth culture, is a place where eccentricity is celebrated. Particularly Takeshita Street is a swirl of colors and fashions. Everything is available, from cosplay shops to Lolita's Gothic clothes. Tokyo rockabilly dancers and other street artists use Harajuku's Yoyogi Park as a stage on Sundays.

6. Respect for Nature in Urban Spaces

Despite being a huge metropolis, Tokyo gives a lot of attention to the outdoors and green areas. A vast park in the middle of the metropolis, Shinjuku Gyoen, provides a peaceful haven from the bustle of the city. Ueno Park, which has a zoo and a number of museums, displays the Japanese reverence for cherry blossoms in the spring.

7. Dining Culture: More Than Just Sushi

Japanese cuisine is a cornerstone of Tokyo's culture, and it goes well beyond sushi. Izakayas (Japanese-style pubs) invite you to savor a wide range of dishes, from yakitori (grilled skewers) to tempura and okonomiyaki (savory pancakes). Tokyo's Tsukiji Fish Market, though relocated to Toyosu, remains a seafood lover's paradise.

Image showing Yakitori

8. Respect and Etiquette

Tokyo is a city where manners and respect for others are deeply engrained. A common way to welcome someone and demonstrate respect is to bow. It is traditional to wash your hands and lips at the purifying fountain before entering temples and shrines.

9. Innovations and Technology

Tokyo's culture goes beyond just history; it also leads the way in technical advancement. From robot eateries in Shinjuku to high-tech toilets that redefine bathroom comfort, you'll come across futuristic encounters. As was already mentioned, Akihabara is a tech mecca where you may discover the newest gadgets and electronics.

Image showing robot receptionist

10. Temples and Shrines in the Urban Jungle

Tokyo is particularly special because it juxtaposes the sacred and secular. Ancient temples and shrines like Meiji Shrine and Senso-ji Temple are in the middle of the city and provide a tranquil sanctuary where you can have spiritual experiences and see customary rituals.

In summary, Tokyo's culture is an intriguing blend of the traditional and the avant-garde, the past and the present. Every street corner, every festival, and every meal in this city offer the chance to learn something new and experience a culture that is both firmly established and constantly changing. So while you go through this beautiful city, embrace the culture, immerse yourself in the traditions, and let Tokyo's special essence charm you.

25 INTERESTING FACTS ABOUT TOKYO

Edo to Tokyo: Tokyo was known as Edo for many years before to the Meiji Restoration in 1868, when it became known as Tokyo.

Kyoto's Claim: Some Kyoto residents still consider Kyoto as the rightful capital of Japan, challenging Tokyo's status.

Robot Hotel: The Hen no Hotel in Ginza, the first robot hotel in the world, is located in Tokyo. Here, robots manage numerous jobs to give guests an unforgettable experience.

Robot Restaurant: You can visit the Robot Restaurant in Shinjuku, a vibrant and energetic destination where tourists are entertained with robot monsters, dancers, and lasers.

Sumo Wrestling: Tokyo stages a number of sumo competitions every year, giving visitors the chance to see this traditional Japanese sport in action.

Population Density: Tokyo is one of the world's most densely populated cities, with more than 13 million people living in just its 23 central districts.

Shibuya Crossing: During rush hour, thousands of people cross the Shibuya Crossing simultaneously, making it one of the busiest pedestrian crossings in the whole world.

Akihabara Electric Town: As the center of Japanese pop culture, electronics, and anime, Akihabara attracts fans from all over the world.

Odaiba Island: The Rainbow Bridge and teamLab Borderless digital art museum may be found on the man-made island of Odaiba in Tokyo Bay, which is well-known for its futuristic design.

Tokyo Disneyland: Tokyo Disneyland was the first Disney park to be built outside the United States and remains one of the most popular attractions in Tokyo.

Yoyogi Park: Previously used as a military parade field, Yoyogi Park is today a well-liked location for gatherings, events, and cosplayers.

Tsukiji Fish Market: The outside Tsukiji Fish Market is still an excellent location to enjoy fresh seafood even though the interior market has relocated to Toyosu.

The Imperial Palace: The historic Edo Castle is now the location of Tokyo's Imperial Palace, which is encircled by lovely gardens.

Historic Asakusa: Asakusa is home to Senso-ji Temple, Tokyo's oldest temple, and Nakamise-dori, a vibrant shopping street.

Skytree Tower: One of the world's highest structures, the Tokyo Skytree provides panoramic views of the city from its observation decks.

Cherry Blossom Festivals: Tokyo's "hanami," or cherry blossom festivals, are celebrated with picnics and events held in parks throughout the city as the cherry trees bloom.

Meiji Shrine: Meiji Shrine is a shrine in Shibuya that honors Emperor Meiji and Empress Shoken and is encircled by serene forest.

Ginza District: Tokyo's upmarket Ginza neighborhood is home to designer boutiques, department stores, and art galleries.

Kawaii Culture: Tokyo is the birthplace of the kawaii (cute) culture, influencing fashion, art, and pop culture around the world.

Capsule Hotels: Tokyo pioneered the idea of capsule hotels, which provide guests with small, cost-effective accommodations.

Harajuku Fashion: Fashion-forward youngsters and visitors alike flock to Harajuku for its unique and unusual street fashion.

Sushi Culture: Tokyo boasts some of the world's finest sushi restaurants, including the iconic Tsukiji Outer Market.

Maid Cafes: Akihabara is famous for its maid cafes, where waitresses dressed as maids provide a playful and immersive dining experience.

Traditional Crafts: Traditional artisans, including those that specialize in pottery, calligraphy, and sword forging, may be found in Tokyo.

Edo-Tokyo Museum: The Edo-Tokyo Museum in Ryogoku provides a captivating journey through the city's history and transformation.

CHAPTER 2

PLANNING YOUR TRIP

WHEN TO VISIT TOKYO

Spring (March to May): Cherry Blossom Season

Spring is arguably the most popular time to visit Tokyo, and for a good reason. Cherry blossom season, known as "sakura" in Japanese, transforms the city into a mesmerizing sea of pink and white blossoms. In full bloom, parks like Ueno, Shinjuku Gyoen, and Chidorigafuchi draw crowds of locals and visitors for picnics and hanami (flower viewing) parties. Depending on the weather, the sakura season normally starts in late March or early April, so planning your trip accordingly can result in a spectacular experience.

Summer (June to August): Festivals and Fireworks

Summer in Tokyo brings vibrant festivals and a lively atmosphere. Traditional celebrations where the night sky comes to life with brilliant fireworks include the Sumida River Fireworks Festival and the Gion Matsuri in Asakusa. Be prepared, though, since it can get rather hot and muggy, especially in July and August. During the summer months, wearing lightweight clothing and drinking plenty of water are vital.

Autumn (September to November): Mild Weather and Fall Foliage

Tokyo's autumn weather is pleasant, and the changing leaves provide beautiful scenery. Autumn foliage is displayed in parks like Meiji Shrine and Showa Memorial Park. In the neighboring mountains, such Mount Takao, September is an excellent time for outdoor activities including trekking. The weather is comfortable, making it an ideal time for sightseeing.

Winter (December to February): Fewer Crowds and Winter Illuminations

When compared to certain other regions of Japan, Tokyo's winters are rather warm, with few nights below freezing. Without the crowds, it is a great time to explore the city. You may immerse yourself in the magnificent winter illuminations that cover Roppongi Hills and Marunouchi Park as well as the streets and parks across Tokyo. Don't forget to warm up with a steaming bowl of ramen or a visit to an onsen (hot spring).

Consider the Holidays and Special Events

Keep in mind that Japanese holidays and special events can impact your travel experience. Peak travel times for the Japanese are Obon (mid-August) and Golden Week (late April to early May), which can make hotels and transportation congested. On the other hand, traveling over New Year's (December 31 to January 1) can offer a distinctive cultural experience as Tokyo's temples and shrines come to life with customary rituals.

Personal Preferences Matter

The ideal time to visit Tokyo ultimately depends on your own tastes. Whether it's the cherry blossoms in spring, the fun festivals in summer, the vibrant leaves in fall, or the hushed charm of winter, each season has its own fascination. Plan your journey taking into account the kind of experience you're looking for.

BUDGETING FOR YOUR TRIP

Planning your budget for a trip to Tokyo is a crucial step to ensure that you have a memorable experience without breaking the bank. Tokyo, while offering a wide range of experiences, can be expensive if you're not careful. Let's explore some practical tips to help you manage your finances and make the most of your trip.

1. Set a Realistic Budget:

Setting a reasonable budget is the first step in creating a budget for your trip to Tokyo. Think about things like how long you want to stay, the kind of accommodations you want, and the amount you intend to spend each day on things like meals, transportation, and entertainment. It's important to be realistic about how much money you can comfortably spend.

2. Cost of Accommodation:

The cost of accommodation in Tokyo can vary greatly. Everything is available, from cheap hostels to five-star hotels. Consider staying in business hotels, guesthouses, or Airbnb rentals to reduce your accommodation costs. When making a reservation, keep an eye out for special deals and discounts.

3. Transportation Costs:

Tokyo's trains and subways are among the city's top-notch public transportation options. Purchase a prepaid transportation card like a Suica or Pasmo card, which provides convenient discounted fares. Consider getting a Japan Rail Pass prior to your trip for unrestricted travel on JR trains if you intend to tour Japan outside of Tokyo.

4. Dining Smart:

Tokyo might be an expensive city to eat out, but there are methods to do it without going broke. For inexpensive dinners, check out the izakayas (local pubs), casual restaurants, and street food stalls. Additionally, take into account restaurant lunch specials, which are sometimes less expensive than dinner.

5. Free and Low-Cost Attractions:

Tokyo has a ton of free and inexpensive attractions. Visit Meiji Shrine and Senso-ji Temple, explore through Ueno Park, and enjoy in the beautiful views from one of Tokyo's numerous observation decks as you explore the thriving neighborhoods. Plan your visits appropriately since many museums offer discounted admission on particular days.

6. Shopping:

While Tokyo is a shopping paradise, it's easy to overspend. Set a shopping budget and stick to it. Look for budget-friendly options like thrift stores, flea markets, and discount shops. Don't forget to claim your tax-free shopping benefits if you meet the criteria.

7. Plan Ahead for Special Experiences:

Allocate a chunk of your money for any special experiences you're looking forward to, such as a sumo match or a traditional tea ceremony. Booking in advance might occasionally result in cost savings.

8. Currency Exchange:

Be aware of currency conversion costs. Using a travel-friendly debit or credit card makes it more affordable to get cash from ATMs in Japan. Notify your bank of your travel plans to avoid card issues.

9. Travel Insurance:

Even if it isn't directly tied to your daily costs, travel insurance is crucial for mental stability. In the event of unforeseen occurrences like trip cancellations, medical problems, or misplaced luggage, it can offer you protection. Think about incorporating it into your budget planning.

10. Flexibility and Contingency:

Last but not least, allow some room in your budget for unforeseen costs or unplanned possibilities that may happen during your vacation. By having a reserve fund, you can avoid being taken off guard.

Keep in mind that sticking to a budget doesn't require sacrificing experiences. During your Tokyo experience, it's important to prioritize what matters most to you and make informed decisions. You may experience Tokyo to the fullest without going overboard with proper planning and a reasonable budget. Safe travels, and may your journey be chock-full of special memories!

TRAVELING TIPS TO TOKYO

1. Learn Basic Japanese Phrases:

Even though many Tokyo residents can communicate in some English, learning a few fundamental Japanese words and expressions will help you establish rapport and make your vacation more enjoyable.

2. Get a Suica or Pasmo Card:

Purchase a prepaid transit card, such as the Suica or Pasmo. Access to Tokyo's large public transportation network, which includes trains, buses, and subways, is made simple with the use of these cards.

3. Respect Local Customs:

In Japan, courtesy and respect are highly valued. In Japan, bowing is a customary greeting, and taking off your shoes is required when entering a person's home or some other places. Talk quietly when in a public place.

4. Tipping is Not Common:

Tipping is not a common practice in Tokyo. Instead, exceptional service is provided as a standard, and tipping can sometimes be considered impolite.

5. Master the Train System:

Although Tokyo's train system can be complicated, it is the most effective and convenient way to travel. To find routes and times, download a train app like HyperDia or Google Maps. Be ready for crowds at rush hour as well.

6. Cash is King:

While credit cards are widely accepted in Tokyo, it's essential to have cash on hand, especially in smaller shops, restaurants, and for transportation.

7. Stay Connected:

Consider renting a pocket Wi-Fi device or purchasing a SIM card at the airport to ensure you have access to the internet and maps while exploring the city.

8. Plan for Seasonal Weather:

In Tokyo, there are four distinct seasons. Examine the weather forecasts for the dates of your trip and pack accordingly. Remember to bring an umbrella because rain is unpredictable.

9. Eat Adventurously:

Try the local cuisine, including sushi, ramen, tempura, and more. Venture beyond your comfort zone and taste some of the unique street foods available at markets and stalls.

10. Sample Japanese Sweets:

Japanese delicacies like mochi, dorayaki, and taiyaki should not be missed. Traditional sweet shops and even some convenience stores carry them.

11. Visit Tourist Information Centers:

At the Narita and Haneda airports, Tokyo offers two tourist information offices. They offer directions, pamphlets, and useful information.

12. Be Punctual:

In Japan, being on time is crucial. Be on time for appointments, reservations, and tours. Buses and trains follow strict schedules as well.

13. Respect No Photography Signs:

Some temples, shrines, and museums may have restrictions on photography or require a fee. Always adhere to the rules and respect the sanctity of these places.

14. Dispose of Trash Properly:

In Tokyo, finding a public trash bin might be difficult. Bring a little bag with you to gather your waste, and when you find a designated trash bin, dispose of it safely.

15. Take Off Your Shoes:

It is customary to take off your shoes at the door when entering traditional ryokans, some eateries, and even some houses. Respect local traditions by following suit.

16. Experience an Onsen:

If you have the chance, indulge in an onsen (hot spring) experience. Japan's geothermal activity provides many opportunities for relaxation and rejuvenation.

17. Be Mindful of Noise:

Keep the volume down, especially at night, in public areas and hotels. Tokyo is a city that treasures peace.

18. Get a JR Pass:

If you plan to explore other parts of Japan, consider purchasing a Japan Rail Pass before your trip. It offers unlimited travel on JR trains and can save you money on long-distance travel.

19. Emergency Numbers:

Know the emergency numbers for Japan. The police can be reached at 110, and medical emergencies at 119.

20. Enjoy Tokyo's Green Spaces:

Tokyo is home to several stunning gardens and parks. Relax in areas like Shinjuku Gyoen or Ueno Park to escape the urban clamor and noise.

These tips will help you navigate Tokyo's distinctive culture and make the most of your vacation. Tokyo is a city with a multitude of things to offer, from ancient temples to cutting-edge technology, and adopting local practices will enhance your trip.

WHERE TO EXCHANGE CURRENCY.

When it comes to exchanging currency in Tokyo, you have several reliable options to choose from, each with its own advantages and considerations. Here's a guide to help you make the most of your currency exchange experience in Japan.

1. Banks and Post Offices: Trustworthy and Convenient

In Tokyo, banks and post offices rank among the safest venues to exchange money. While they have reasonable charges, you should be aware that there will be some paperwork to fill out, which could take 15 to 30 minutes. But these organizations offer a safe and regulated environment for cash exchange.

2. Licensed Money Changers: Competitive Rates

In Japan, authorized money changers are renowned for their competitive prices. They may not be as widespread as banks and post offices, but if you're looking for better rates and quicker service, they can be an excellent choice. Licensed money changers who are trustworthy and reputed offer a hassle-free experience.

3. Kinken Shops: A Unique Option

Kinken shops, which typically deal in unused event tickets, can also serve as currency exchange points. While not as common as other options, they can offer good rates. Daikokuya is one of the most prominent and trusted kinken shop chains in Tokyo, providing reliable currency exchange services.

4. Currency Exchange Machines: Quick and Convenient

Although not common, currency exchange machines can be found in well-known tourist locations, shopping malls, and significant railroad stations. These devices perform an ATM-like function, however they only exchange currency. Insert your foreign cash, and it will automatically dispense the corresponding amount in Japanese Yen (JPY). Machines that exchange money are renowned for being quick and simple to operate.

5. ATM Machines: Preferred by Many Travelers

In Tokyo, using ATMs is frequently the preferred way to get Japanese Yen. It is unnecessary to carry significant amounts of foreign currency because ATM rates are normally competitive. To avoid any problems, be careful to let your local bank know that you intend to use your ATM card overseas. Although some ATMs accept ATM cards, it is recommended to use 7-Eleven and post office ATMs for the best success rate.

Important Tip: Opt for "Without Conversion"

In Japan, there is a possibility that you will be given the choice to proceed "with or without conversion." To have your local bank handle the currency conversion, always select "WITHOUT conversion". Selecting "with conversion" gives the foreign bank operating the ATM permission to do the conversion, frequently at unfavorable rates. To get the best value for your money, choose "without conversion" because the rate difference can be as much as 10%.

To sum up, Tokyo has a wide range of reliable choices for currency conversion, from conventional banks and post offices to authorized money changers, kinken stores, currency exchange machines, and ATMs. Each choice offers benefits, so pick the one that most closely matches your requirements and tastes to make sure you get the most out of your currency exchange during your trip to this vibrant city.

JAPAN VISA

Depending on your passport and the purpose of your visit, you might be required to obtain a visa and fulfill specific entry requirements when planning a trip to Japan. We suggest visiting iVisa.com to get detailed information about the visa requirements that relate to your particular situation. This portal offers a simplified visa application service in addition to useful information about the required paperwork and procedures, making sure that your travel preparations are easy and hassle-free.

The visa application procedure can occasionally be confusing, especially when entrance requirements differ depending on your nationality and the reason for your stay. Therefore, it might be very beneficial to consult a trustworthy website like iVisa.com to make sure you have all the required paperwork in place.

It's essential to keep up with the most recent criteria and requirements for visas because they can change over time. Additionally, the particular visa category and supporting documentation may vary based on the purpose of your travel, such as whether it is for business, pleasure, or research. Use online tools like iVisa.com to speed up your application process and confirm the most recent visa criteria to prevent any potential delays or problems during your journey planning.

Making travel arrangements to Japan is an exciting activity, and making sure you comply with all entry and visa regulations is essential to a hassle-free and enjoyable trip. You may receive helpful information and support to make sure you are well-prepared for your future voyage in the Land of the Rising Sun by using dependable platforms like iVisa.com.

MONEY-SAVING TIPS FOR TRAVELERS IN TOKYO

Tokyo, often recognized as one of the world's pricier destinations, can still be a budget-friendly adventure with the right strategies. By incorporating these money-saving tips into your Tokyo travel plan, you can experience this vibrant city without breaking the bank, enjoying inexpensive dining, affordable activities, and savvy choices on transportation and accommodation.

1. Public Transportation Over Taxis:

Taxis in Tokyo start at 475 JPY, making them an expensive option for daily commuting. Choose public transportation instead. Tokyo's wide network of routes for the metro runs till midnight. If you can return before that time, JR East offers more affordable options with trains running until 1:20 am.

2. 100-Yen Stores for Necessities:

Discover Tokyo's equivalent of dollar stores, known as 100-yen shops. These stores offer a variety of essentials, including premade meals, groceries, toiletries, and household items, all at budget-friendly prices. Simply inquire at your accommodation for the nearest "Hyaku En" shop.

3. Inexpensive Dining Options:

Take into account eating at convenience stores like 7-Eleven and Family Mart, which provide a cost-effective lunch option by selling meal sets for under 500 JPY. Additionally, supermarkets offer affordable food options. Discover regional specialties like curry, ramen, and donburi at important bus or train terminals, where inexpensive meals are often available.

4. Get a Transportation Pass:

Purchase a transit day pass or prepaid card because you'll probably need it to get about the city. Tokyo provides a range of passes to meet the needs of various railway and metro operators. One-day passes normally cost between 600 and 1,600 JPY, saving the buyer a lot of money over buying individual tickets.

5. Tokyo Museum Grutto Pass:

The Tokyo Museum Grutto Pass, which costs only 2,500 JPY, is an excellent purchase if you intend to visit several of Tokyo's museums and attractions. You have access to 101 museums and attractions with this card. Additionally, it can be purchased as a digital ticket to simplify your museum visits.

6. Connect with Locals:

Use websites like Couchsurfing to meet local hosts and receive free accommodation as well as insights into daily life in Tokyo. Start your enquiries early because such platforms' response times can be long. Since they are typically more active on these networks, consider contacting expats.

7. Exchange Work for Accommodation:

In certain hostels in Tokyo, you may earn your room by working. Typically, in exchange for a free hotel room, you might spend a few hours cleaning in the morning. Find out in advance if any hostels will be providing this budget-friendly choice throughout your intended stay.

8. Capsule Hotels for Budget Stays:

Travelers on a tight budget have a more economical option than typical hostels with capsule hotels. Although the amenities may be more basic, they provide an affordable option for resting in Tokyo without sacrificing comfort.

9. Shop Smart for Fresh Food:

Shop at supermarkets after 8 p.m. to benefit from savings on fresh groceries. By saving up to 50% on fresh goods, this evening's special enables you to cook cost-effective meals while here.

10. Carry a Reusable Water Bottle:

Tokyo's tap water is safe to drink, making it unnecessary to buy bottled water. Bring a reusable water bottle to save money and reduce plastic waste. Brands like LifeStraw offer bottles with built-in filters, ensuring clean and safe drinking water throughout your journey.

You'll not only make the most of your budget by implementing these cost-cutting suggestions into your Tokyo travel itinerary, but you'll also open up possibilities to fully immerse yourself in the culture and experiences that this vibrant city has to offer. Tokyo is calling, and with some careful budgeting, your trip may be both economical and enjoyable.

CHAPTER 3

GETTING AROUND TOKYO

NAVIGATING TOKYO'S TRANSPORTATION

Navigating Tokyo's transportation system might seem intimidating at first, given its vastness and complexity, but fear not – it's one of the most efficient and reliable systems in the world. Here's a guide to help you navigate Tokyo's transportation and get around the city like a pro.

Trains and Subways: The Heart of Tokyo's Transport

Tokyo's transportation system is based on trains and subways. Most of the lines are run by JR East and the Tokyo Metro. Invest in a prepaid transit card like a Pasmo or Suica card, which offers easy access to buses, trains, subways, and even some taxis. The fastest and most economical way to travel about Tokyo is by rail or metro, which have a vast network that reaches every part of the city.

Navigating the Subway Lines:

Tokyo's subway lines are color-coded and numbered, making them relatively easy to navigate. English signage and station announcements are common, but it's helpful to have a navigation app (like HyperDia or Google Maps) to plan your routes and check train schedules.

Rush Hour Considerations:

Tokyo's peak periods, particularly the morning and evening commutes, can be congested. To guarantee a more comfortable trip, try to avoid traveling during these busy hours.

Buses and Trams: An Alternative Option

Buses and trams are great for getting to places that aren't easily reached by train. Due to traffic, they could take a little longer, but they offer a unique way to see other areas. When boarding, pay for your travel with your Suica or Pasmo card, and make sure to research bus routes and schedules beforehand.

Taxis: For Convenience and Privacy

Tokyo's taxis are clean, secure, and comfortable, although they might be more expensive than other forms of public transportation. Taxis are especially useful when you have heavy luggage or when public transportation isn't convenient. Taxis are easily accessible and can be found at taxi stands or flagged down on the street.

Walking and Cycling: Exploring at a Leisurely Pace

Tokyo is a city that encourages pedestrians, and numerous attractions are close to one another. Walking is a great way to experience the culture and find hidden gems. To get a different perspective of the city, think about hiring a bike from one of Tokyo's many bike-sharing services.

Transportation Apps and Resources:

Use route-planning programs like Google Maps or HyperDia to look up current schedules and plan your travels. These apps seamlessly integrate with Tokyo's huge public transportation network, making it simple to find the best routes and estimated arrival times.

Accessibility Considerations:

The majority of Tokyo's major stations feature ramps, elevators, and restrooms that are accessible if you have mobility issues. Japan is working harder than ever to make travel easier for everyone.

Language Barrier:

While many signs and announcements are in English, some stations and bus routes may have limited English information. Having your destination written in Japanese or using a translation app can be immensely helpful.

Tokyo's Transportation IC Cards:

It's important to keep in mind that Suica and Pasmo cards can be used for a variety of services, including buying at convenience stores, using vending machines, and even taking select taxis.

You'll find travelling around this vibrant metropolis to be a snap with a little planning and some familiarity with Tokyo's transit alternatives. Accept the challenge and let Tokyo's reliable and effective transportation system be your pass to discovering all that this amazing city has to offer. Travel safely!

TOKYO METRO AND JR PASS

Tokyo Metro and JR Pass are two essential components of Tokyo's extensive public transportation system, each serving a unique purpose for travelers exploring the city and its surrounding regions.

Tokyo Metro: Navigating the City with Precision

The city's subway system, known as the Tokyo Metro, is recognized for its punctuality and effectiveness. It has nine lines and covers almost all of Tokyo, making it easy to get to popular attractions, neighborhoods, and retail areas. Tokyo Metro lines are numbered and color-coded to make navigating easier for both locals and visitors.

Image showing passengers traveling by Tokyo Metro

The Tokyo Metro is a great option for tourists who want to quickly commute between the city's major hubs, including Shibuya, Shinjuku, and Ginza. It's a reliable means to go to famous locations like the Tokyo Tower, the Senso-ji Temple in Asakusa, and the fashionable Harajuku neighborhood. Tokyo Metro also provides a variety of ticket choices, including one-day passes and multi-day cards, giving you flexibility for your travel requirements.

JR Pass: Explore Beyond Tokyo

Travelers who want to see other areas of Japan in addition to Tokyo might consider the Japan Rail Pass, also known as the JR Pass. This pass, which is run by JR (Japan Railways), allows unrestricted travel for a predetermined number of consecutive days on JR trains, buses, and even some ferries.

Although you can use the JR Pass inside of Tokyo, its true worth is seen when you travel outside of the city. The JR Pass is an affordable option for those looking to see several areas of Japan because it makes it simple to explore places like Kyoto, Osaka, Hiroshima, and more. The pass is offered in a various periods, often ranging from 7 to 21 days, to accommodate varied travel itineraries.

Plan your interstate trips and reserve seats on the well-liked Shinkansen (bullet trains) in advance to get the most out of your JR Pass discounts; these trains can get crowded, particularly during the peak travel times.

The JR Pass, which opens up a world of travel options outside the city and is a need for anyone wishing to discover the greater delights of Japan, is your go-to pick for precisely traversing Tokyo's popular neighborhoods and attractions. Both alternatives are practical and accessible, enabling you to get the most out of your trip across Tokyo and the stunning areas outside its limits.

BIKING AND WALKING IN TOKYO

While Tokyo is renowned for its advanced transportation system, there's a quieter, more leisurely side to the city that's best explored on foot or by bicycle. Here's a glimpse into the joys of biking and walking in Tokyo:

Walking in Tokyo: Unveiling Hidden Gems

Walking is a fantastic method to discover Tokyo's heart and spirit. The areas of the city are teeming with interesting streets, ancient sites, and bustling markets that are just waiting to be discovered. You'll see the clash of old and new as you stroll through the busy streets, with contemporary buildings rising next to traditional wooden homes and historic temples.

Senso-ji Temple in Asakusa: A leisurely walk through Nakamise-dori, the shopping street leading to Senso-ji Temple, allows you to soak in the atmosphere and savor street snacks like freshly made ningyo-yaki (sweet red bean cakes).

Yanaka District: Yanaka, a district well-known for its preserved Edo-era atmosphere, is best explored on foot. Explore the artisan shops, shrines, and traditional homes that line its winding streets.

Meiji Shrine: Shibuya's approach to Meiji Shrine offers a tranquil respite from the city's bustle with its tall torii gate and forested path, making it the ideal place for a reflective stroll.

Biking in Tokyo: A Unique Perspective

Consider renting a bicycle to tour Tokyo in a more efficient and active way. Tokyo's rental and bike-sharing facilities make it simple to pedal throughout the city, providing a distinctive viewpoint on its varied districts and attractions.

Tokyo Bay Area: Hire a bike at Odaiba and tour the beautiful Tokyo Bay region, where you can take in breath-taking vistas of the Rainbow Bridge and the cutting-edge Palette Town architecture.

Cycling along the Sumida River: Follow the Sumida River cycling path, which winds through parks and bridges, allowing you to take in both the natural beauty and urban landscapes along the way.

Ueno Park and Yanaka: Explore Ueno Park's vast grounds on two wheels before going neighboring Yanaka district for a more in-depth exploration to combine biking and walking.

Safety and Convenience

Biking and walking in Tokyo are not only enjoyable but also safe and convenient. The city prioritizes pedestrian-friendly infrastructure, with well-maintained sidewalks, crosswalks, and pedestrian bridges. Cyclists can take advantage of designated bike lanes and parking areas throughout the city.

Renting Bicycles: Electric bikes are available in many bike rental shops, and they can assist you easily navigate Tokyo's hills. To ensure your safety, you must abide by local traffic laws, wear a helmet if necessary, and use lights at night.

Navigating on Foot: Putting on a pair of suitable walking shoes and stepping out are all that are required to navigate Tokyo on foot. You can use navigation apps to help you find your way, but occasionally getting a little lost in Tokyo's maze-like alleys can result in delightful discoveries.

Cultural Immersion: Walking and biking both present chances for cultural immersion. Interacting with locals, finding small, family-run businesses, and stumbling onto quaint cafes and eateries hidden away in quiet corners are all possible.

Walking and riding both offer distinctive perspectives on this vibrant city, whether you prefer to stroll around Tokyo's ancient districts, visit famous monuments on foot, or set out on a bicycle excursion. So, put on your favorite walking shoes or saddle up your bike and go off to explore Tokyo's hidden gems at your own leisure.

TRAVELLING TO TOKYO AND GETTING AROUND.

Traveling to Tokyo: Navigating Your Arrival

Planning your trip to Tokyo is a thrilling first step toward discovering this dynamic city. Tokyo greets you with open arms whether you are traveling from outside or within Japan. Here is a thorough guide to assist you get around once you arrive in Tokyo. It includes insights and suggestions to make getting around to your destination as easy as possible.

Arrival via Narita International Airport (NRT)

One of the main entry points for international passengers is Narita International Airport, which is located roughly 65 kilometers east of central Tokyo. From there, you have a few alternatives for getting to the city's center:

1. Metro from Narita Terminals 1 and 2:

Narita Terminals 1 and 2 have convenient metro stations in their basements. For those arriving at Terminal 3, a free shuttle bus is available to transport you to Terminal 2, where you can access the metro system.

2. JR Narita Express (N'EX):

The fastest way to get from Narita to Tokyo Station is on the JR Narita Express, which travels there in about an hour. This is a great choice if you intend to use a JR Pass because it is entirely covered by the pass.

3. JR Sobu Line (Rapid):

61

Although it takes the JR Sobu Line around 90 minutes to get to Tokyo Station, it is a more reasonable option for those on a tighter budget than the Narita Express.

4. Keisei Skyliner:

In around 40 minutes, the Keisei Skyliner will take you to Nippori Station, where you can connect to your final destination. To save time, think about buying your tickets in advance, separately or as part of a Tokyo Subway Ticket package.

5. Keisei Limited Express:

The Keisei Limited Express, though slower than the Skyliner, offers an economical option, taking approximately 75 minutes to reach Nippori Station.

6. Bus Options:

For those preferring a bus transfer, the Limousine Bus offers direct routes to Tokyo Station and several major hotels in central Tokyo. Alternatively, the "Airport Bus TYO-NRT" takes you to either Tokyo Station or Ginza Station in about 90 minutes.

7. Private/Shared Transfer or Taxi:

While handy, private and shared shuttle options from Narita Airport to central Tokyo are more expensive. Despite being widely available, taxis are the most expensive choice.

Arrival via Haneda Airport (HND)

Haneda Airport, located about 17 kilometers south of central Tokyo, is another major international entry point. To reach your destination within Tokyo:

1. Tokyo Monorail:

Haneda Airport and Hamamatsucho Station are connected by the Tokyo Monorail in around 20 minutes. You may easily board a connecting train from there to get to your destination.

2. Keikyu Railways:

In roughly 20 minutes, the Keikyu Airport Line takes passengers to Shinagawa Station, where they can change to their preferred form of transportation to get to their accommodation.

3. Limousine Bus:

Much like at Narita, the Limousine Bus service is available at Haneda Airport. You can check if your hotel is on the serviced route list.

4. Private/Shared Transfer or Taxi:

From Haneda Airport to central Tokyo, there are private and shared shuttle options available for your convenience. Taxis are another alternative, though rates can change based on where you're going and the time of day.

Arrival from Other Parts of Japan

Traveling to Tokyo by rail is frequently the most effective and practical choice if your trip begins in another city in Japan. Because of its excellent rail infrastructure, Japan is a popular destination for intercity travel. Use the Hyperdia search engine to locate the most accurate and dependable rail routes to Tokyo from any location in Japan.

Consider the Japan Rail Pass (JR Pass) if you plan on exploring multiple regions in Japan. It offers unlimited travel on JR trains for the duration of your pass, providing excellent value for frequent travelers.

In conclusion, Tokyo provides a variety of access points and modes of transportation to suit the needs of a wide range of visitors. When you have the appropriate information, you can easily start your Tokyo experience as soon as you land at Narita International Airport or Haneda Airport. The allure of Tokyo is waiting for you, promising life-changing encounters and enduring memories. Travel safely!

CHAPTER 4

TOKYO'S NEIGHBORHOODS AND TOP DESTINATIONS

SHINJUKU: THE HEART OF TOKYO

When it comes to the vibrant tapestry of Tokyo's neighborhoods, few places capture the city's essence and energy quite like Shinjuku. Nestled at the heart of this sprawling metropolis, Shinjuku is a microcosm of Tokyo's past, present, and future, offering travelers a kaleidoscope of experiences that define the Japanese capital.

A Dynamic Hub of Contrasts

In the neighborhood of Shinjuku, tradition and modernity coexist together. Towering skyscrapers that appear to reach the clouds will meet you as you enter the city's busy streets, representing Tokyo's futuristic cityscape. But right around the corner, you'll find quaint lanes and ancient corners that honor the city's Edo-era origins.

Shinjuku Gyoen National Garden: A Serene Oasis

Shinjuku Gyoen National Garden is a quiet haven amidst the metropolitan bustle and neon lights. This finely designed park provides a break from the hectic pace of the city. It's a refuge for watching cherry blossoms in the spring and a tranquil retreat all year long. Take a stroll through gardens that showcase the beauty of nature, such as those in Japan, France, and England.

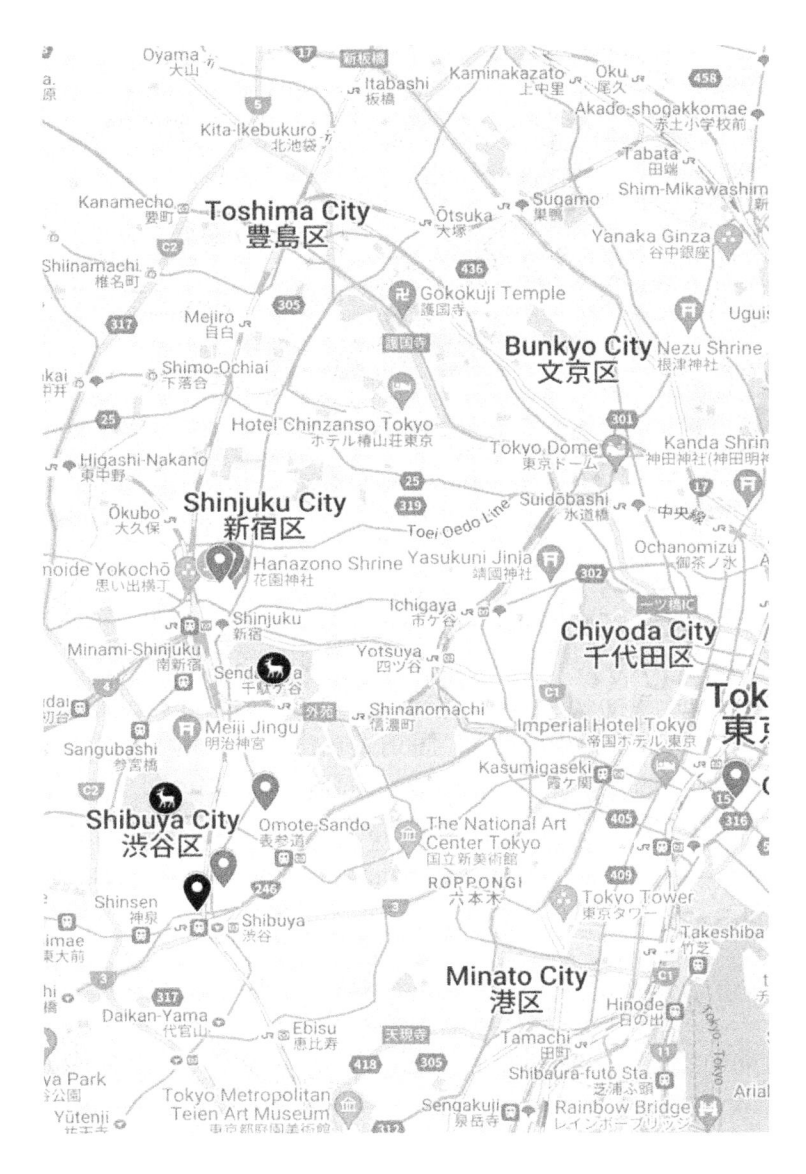

https://www.google.com/maps/d/u/0/edit?mid=1z60QUaH
Ld6Jqx6LbWRThNxnG07EsoZM&ll=35.69333638372339
%2C139.72605811710204&z=15

Kabukicho: Neon Wonderland

Tokyo's nightlife comes to life in Kabukicho, the center of the neighborhood's entertainment scene. As you explore the numerous bars, clubs, and entertainment options, neon signs brighten the night. While Kabukicho is well-known for its thriving nightlife, it also has a variety of unique restaurants, izakayas (traditional Japanese pubs), and odd boutiques that entice tourists.

Shinjuku Station: A Transport Hub

The station at Shinjuku is a world unto itself. It demonstrates Tokyo's effectiveness as one of the busiest transit hubs in the world. Beyond its role as a transit point, the station's underground labyrinth houses a plethora of dining, shopping, and entertainment options, making it easy to lose track of time exploring its depths.

Golden Gai: A Nostalgic Enclave

Wander around Golden Gai, a collection of modest bars lining narrow alleyways, and travel back in time. Each bar has its own distinct personality. This nostalgic neighborhood provides a close-up view of Tokyo's past in sharp contrast to the district's contemporary façade.

Skyscraper District: Iconic Views

The western district of Shinjuku is a haven for those who enjoy architecture and expansive views. A free observation deck with stunning views of Tokyo is available at the Tokyo Metropolitan Government Building, one of the district's prominent towers. The opulent Park Hyatt Tokyo, which was nearby and featured in the movie "Lost in Translation," offers a chic location for cocktails with a view.

Shopping Extravaganza:

Shinjuku is a shopping haven for all tastes and budgets. There is something for every consumer, from high-end brands in the luxurious department stores of Shinjuku Southern Terrace to unique items at the Omoide Yokocho (Memory Lane) market. Don't forget to look for hidden treasures in the Shinjuku Underground Shopping Arcade's underground wonderland.

Friendly Locals and Immersive Experiences

Shinjuku's biggest advantage is its people, not its attractions. Engage in discussion with locals at inviting cafes, share a meal at an izakaya, or at the lively food stands. Shinjuku residents are renowned for their cordial friendliness and readiness to show visitors about their preferred neighborhood.

As you become more engrossed in the diverse world of Shinjuku, you'll discover that this neighborhood is more than simply a location on a map; it's also an ever-evolving story of Tokyo's past, present, and future. Shinjuku captures the essence of Tokyo—a city of wonderful contrasts and limitless discovery—with its calm parks, neon-lit avenues, historic nooks, and futuristic skyscrapers. Here you are in the center of Tokyo.

SHIBUYA: TOKYO'S TRENDSETTING DISTRICT

Shibuya, the iconic neighborhood of Tokyo, is a bustling urban playground that pulsates with youthful energy, creative trends, and an unbridled spirit of individuality. Known worldwide for its vibrant street culture and iconic pedestrian scramble, Shibuya is Tokyo's trendsetting district that captures the essence of modern Japan.

Shibuya Crossing: A World-Famous Intersection

When you think of Shibuya, you automatically picture the renowned Shibuya Crossing, a fascinating display of organized chaos. A surprising flood of pedestrians surges in all directions every time the traffic lights change, creating a kaleidoscope of action. This famous crossroads is a must-see for all tourists and embodies Tokyo's frantic energy.

Fashion Forward: Shopping in Shibuya

Shibuya is Tokyo's epicenter of fashion and style. The area is home to many boutiques showing the most recent trends in streetwear, high fashion, and everything in between, as well as the flagship stores of numerous international companies. Discover Shibuya 109, a haven for youthful fashionistas, or browse the eccentric shops in the Ura-Harajuku area for one-of-a-kind items.

Harajuku: A Subculture Wonderland

Shibuya's neighboring Harajuku neighborhood is a hotspot for alternative fashion and teenage subcultures. Particularly Takeshita Street is a sensory overload of eccentric stores, themed eateries, and vivid street art. Avant-garde fashion movements like Gothic Lolita, Visual Kei, and Kawaii culture all have their origins in Harajuku.

Yoyogi Park: Tranquil Respite

Yoyogi Park provides a peaceful haven amidst the urban turmoil. This vast green sanctuary, which served as the venue for the 1964 Olympics, entices with its beautiful grass, tranquil ponds, and tall trees. Picnics, leisurely strolls, and cultural activities are all popular there. The park holds lively street events on Sundays that draw musicians, dancers, and painters.

Cultural Enclaves: Art and Music

Shibuya is also home to vibrant cultural enclaves. Get your fill of art and culture at the Bunkamura complex, which features theaters, galleries, and live events. Visit venues like Shibuya O-EAST, known for showcasing up-coming local talent and international acts, to learn more about the live music scene.

Culinary Delights: Shibuya's Food Scene

As diversified as its fashion scene is Shibuya's cuisine scene. Enjoy cosmopolitan delicacies at the various restaurants lining the streets, or indulge in traditional Japanese food at izakayas. Don't miss on Shibuya's delicious street cuisine, including the savory takoyaki and the sweet taiyaki.

Shibuya by Night: Neon Lights and Nightlife

Shibuya becomes a brilliant display of neon lights and a vibrant nightlife when the sun sets. Discover the lively taverns, clubs, and nightclubs in the area, each with an own ambience. There is something for every taste in Shibuya's famed nightlife, which ranges from cozy jazz pubs to energetic nightclubs.

Shibuya's Cultural Influence

Shibuya has a significant cultural impact outside of its immediate city. It's a place where originality has no limitations and where fashion trends for the entire world are established. Shibuya has an ongoing influence on global pop culture, from the eccentric street wear to the vibrant music scene.

Shibuya: Where Past and Future Converge

Shibuya encapsulates Tokyo's dynamic spirit—where past and future converge in a dazzling display of creativity and innovation. Whether you're a fashion aficionado, an art enthusiast, or simply a traveler seeking to soak in Tokyo's contemporary essence, Shibuya is a district that promises a memorable and trendsetting experience. Welcome to Shibuya, where the pulse of Tokyo beats at its most vibrant.

ASAKUSA: TRADITION MEETS MODERNITY

Asakusa, a district nestled along the eastern banks of the Sumida River, is a captivating blend of Tokyo's rich cultural heritage and its ever-evolving modernity. It's a place where echoes of the past coexist peacefully with modern advancements, giving visitors a view into both Japan's past and its thriving modern culture.

Senso-ji Temple: A Gateway to Tradition

Senso-ji Temple, Tokyo's oldest and most recognizable Buddhist temple, is located in the center of Asakusa. After passing through the massive Thunder Gate (Kaminarimon), which is marked by a huge red lantern, you will arrive on Nakamise-dori, a busy street packed with traditional vendors selling a variety of trinkets and street foods. It's a sensory journey that transports you to a bygone era.

Asakusa neighborhood

Tokyo's Asakusa neighborhood, located on the eastern bank of the Sumida River, is a fascinating synthesis of the city's rich cultural history with its dynamic modernity. It's a location where remnants of the past coexist peacefully with modern advancements, giving visitors a view into both Japan's past and its thriving modern culture.

Asakusa Culture and Tourist Information Center: Modern Skyline Views

Ascend the Asakusa Culture and Tourist Information Center for a startling contrast to the temple's medieval allure. From its viewing deck, you can see the contemporary skyline of Tokyo, with distant monuments like the Tokyo Skytree. It's a striking example of how Asakusa successfully combines the old with the new.

Sumida Aquarium: An Underwater Experience

Venture to Tokyo Skytree Town, adjacent to Asakusa, where you'll find the Sumida Aquarium. You can get up close and personal with marine life from Tokyo Bay in this cutting-edge aquatic fantasy, which will immerse you in a beautiful underwater world.

Traditional Festivals: Matsuri and Hanabi

Japanese festivals are synonymous with Asakusa. The annual Sumida River Fireworks Festival (Sumidagawa Hanabi Taikai) has a spectacular fireworks display that draws people from all around the world. You can also see processions, music, and dancing in a vivid celebration of tradition during the Sanja Matsuri, one of Tokyo's biggest and rowdiest festivals.

Asakusa Rox Shopping Complex: Modern Retail Therapy

Visit Asakusa Rox, a cutting-edge shopping center next to Senso-ji Temple, for a contemporary shopping experience. Here, you may indulge in clothing, accessories, and a variety of culinary options while taking in a view of the busy streets below.

Cultural Workshops: Experiencing Traditions

You may interact with traditional Japanese arts and crafts at Asakusa. Take part in tea ceremonies, calligraphy classes, or even try your hand at making a ningyo, a type of traditional Japanese doll. These encounters give a stronger link to Japan's cultural roots.

Asakusa: Bridging the Past and Present

Asakusa embodies the essence of Tokyo's enduring charm—a district where ancient customs and contemporary living coexist harmoniously. It's a location where the architectural tranquility of Senso-ji Temple meets the contemporary energy of Tokyo Skytree. Asakusa welcomes you with open arms and invites you to cross the bridge between tradition and modernity, whether you're looking for a taste of Japanese history, a look at its contemporary innovations, or a blend of both. Welcome to Asakusa, where time-honored heritage meets the vitality of today.

AKIHABARA: Tokyo's Electrifying Nerve Center

Akihabara, often referred to as "Akiba" by locals, is a district in Tokyo that pulsates with the vibrant energy of technology, pop culture, and a distinctive otaku subculture. It's a place where the future unfolds amid neon lights and anime-inspired wonders, making it an absolute must-visit neighborhood for tech enthusiasts, gamers, and anyone curious about Japan's contemporary culture.

Electric Town: Tech Paradise

Electric Town, a haven for tech enthusiasts, can be found in the center of Akihabara. You can discover multistory electronics stores here that are packed with the newest technology, including laptops, cameras, and other devices. Akihabara is a mecca for tech-savvy tourists, offering everything from cutting-edge smartphones to old-school video game systems.

Anime and Manga Galore: Otaku Culture

Akihabara is the epicenter of Japan's otaku culture, celebrating anime and manga in all their forms. Stores dedicated to anime merchandise, figurines, and collectibles line the streets, showcasing characters from beloved series. It's a place where fans can immerse themselves in the world of their favorite shows and characters.

Maid Cafés: Unique Dining Experience

Visit one of the renowned maid cafés in Akihabara for a totally unique dining experience. In this restaurant, waitstaff costumed as maids or anime characters offer a fun and engaging dining experience. It's an exceptional chance to eat well and drink well while being entertained by the friendly personnel.

Retro Gaming: Nostalgic Delights

Gamers will appreciate Akihabara's dedication to retro gaming. Specialty shops offer a diverse collection of vintage consoles, classic games, and rare finds. Whether you're searching for a childhood favorite or a rare gem, Akihabara has it covered.

Cosplay Culture: Dress the Part

Cosplay is encouraged in Akihabara as a form of self-expression. Visitors can become their favorite characters by renting costumes and other props from local businesses. Cosplayers are frequently seen wandering the streets or posing for pictures in designated areas.

Maid Cafés: Unique Dining Experience

Visit one of the renowned maid cafés in Akihabara for a totally unique dining experience. In this restaurant, waitstaff costumed as maids or anime characters offer a fun and engaging dining experience. It's an exceptional chance to eat well and drink well while being entertained by the welcoming personnel.

Events and Festivals: Otaku Celebrations

Throughout the year, Akihabara organizes a number of celebrations and festivals honoring various facets of otaku culture. These events, which range from anime screenings and gaming competitions to cosplay parties, provide you the chance to interact with other enthusiasts and really experience the subculture.

Modern Innovations: Tokyo Skytree

Tokyo Skytree, one of the tallest broadcasting towers in the world, is easily accessible from Akihabara. This modern marvel offers breathtaking panoramic views of Tokyo and beyond. It serves as evidence of Tokyo's ongoing blending of modernity and tradition.

Akihabara: The Nexus of Modernity

In addition to being a neighborhood, Akihabara is a cultural phenomenon that symbolizes Japan's ongoing development. It's a place where cutting-edge technology coexists with nostalgic treasures, where fantasy blends seamlessly with reality. Whether you're a tech enthusiast, an anime aficionado, or simply curious about the contemporary face of Tokyo, Akihabara is the buzzing nerve center where innovation and imagination meet. Welcome to Akihabara, where the future is here and the possibilities are endless.

GINZA

Ginza, often regarded as Tokyo's luxury playground, is a district that exudes sophistication, glamour, and extravagance. It's a neighborhood where shopping reaches unparalleled heights, where haute couture mingles with cutting-edge technology, and where culinary delights rival the finest in the world. Here, every street corner is adorned with the promise of indulgence and elegance.

High-End Shopping: Retail Paradise

Ginza is known for its upscale stores. High-end department stores, designer shops, and the flagship locations of well-known brands may all be found in the area. As you walk the streets, you will come across brands like Chanel, Louis Vuitton, and Dior. The department stores in Ginza, like Mitsukoshi and Wako, are true retail palaces that display the best of both Japanese and international fashion.

UNIQLO Flagship Store: Iconic Shopping

UNIQLO enthusiasts will be delighted to explore the 12-floor flagship store in Ginza, UNIQLO's largest to date. It's a testament to Tokyo's retail innovation, offering a vast array of stylish yet affordable clothing. From fashion-forward apparel to functional basics, this flagship store has it all.

Culinary Excellence: Dining Gems

Ginza is a gourmet wonderland as well as a center for fashion. There are several good dining establishments in the area, each with unique culinary specialties. Take a culinary journey with modern Japanese fusion, indulge in sushi made by skilled chefs, or savor traditional kaiseki food. The gastronomic scene in Ginza is evidence of Japan's dedication to culinary excellence.

Tsukiji Outer Market: Culinary Exploration

The famed fish and seafood haven of Tokyo, Tsukiji Outer Market, is just a short 15-minute walk from Ginza. Here, you may go on a culinary adventure and sample delicious seafood dishes including fresh sushi and sashimi. It is evidence of the variety and excellence of Japan's culinary riches.

Cultural Experiences: The Kabuki Theater

The Kabuki-za Theater in Ginza provides a taste of traditional Japanese theatrical arts. Experience captivating kabuki performances that have mesmerized people for generations. Ginza's ability to smoothly combine history and innovation can be seen in the theater's architecture, which is a blend of traditional and modern design.

Nightlife: Bars and Lounges

As the sun sets, Ginza transforms into a hub of nightlife. Explore the district's chic bars and lounges, each offering a unique atmosphere and crafted cocktails. It's a place to unwind and toast to the day's discoveries in style.

Art Galleries and Museums: Creative Pursuits

Ginza offers a variety of galleries and museums that emphasize modern Japanese and foreign art for art enthusiasts. Investigate exhibitions that stretch the limits of imagination and creativity.

Ginza: The Epitome of Elegance

Ginza is more than just a district; it is also an example of Japanese perfection, the epitome of elegance, and a celebration of luxury. Shopping for the most luxurious clothing, indulging in the finest cuisine, or immersing yourself in the arts—Ginza promises an experience unlike any other. It is the meeting point between innovation and splendor in Tokyo, where every moment is a celebration of life's luxuries. Welcome to Ginza, where splurging knows no bounds, dining is a thrill, and buying is an art.

CHAPTER 5

TOP ATTRACTIONS IN TOKYO YOU SHOULD VISIT

TOKYO DISNEYLAND AND DISNEYSEA

Tokyo Disneyland and Tokyo DisneySea are two enchanting theme parks that capture the imagination of visitors of all ages. Situated in Urayasu, just a short train ride from central Tokyo, these parks offer a magical escape into the world of Disney, where dreams take flight, and enchantment awaits.

Tokyo Disneyland: Classic Disney Magic

You'll enter Tokyo Disneyland and be transported to a world where beloved Disney characters come to life. The World Bazaar and Cinderella Castle are the two primary areas of the park, and each has its own special attractions and experiences to offer.

World Bazaar: Stroll down the charming streets of the World Bazaar, reminiscent of a turn-of-the-century American town. Here, you can shop for Disney merchandise, savor delicious snacks, and enjoy classic Disney rides like "It's a Small World" and "The Enchanted Tiki Room."

Cinderella Castle: The famous Cinderella Castle dominates the park's middle, beckoning guests to explore its enchanted interior and take in its thrilling stage shows and parades.

Tokyo DisneySea: A World of Imagination

Tokyo DisneySea is a unique theme park that takes you to a fantastical and adventurous world. It is located just next to Tokyo Disneyland. It is separated into seven places of call, each with a different theme and enticing attractions.

https://www.google.com/maps/d/u/0/edit?mid=1z60QUaH
Ld6Jqx6LbWRThNxnG07EsoZM&ll=35.6786426588786
%2C139.72455478506902&z=14

Mediterranean Harbor: Start your journey at Mediterranean Harbor, where Disney magic and the magnificence of the Mediterranean meet. Dont miss up the incredible "Fantasmic!" nightly spectacle that takes place on the harbor's waters.

American Waterfront: Step back in time to early 20th-century America at the American Waterfront. Ride the romantic "Venetian Gondolas" or embark on an undersea adventure with Captain Nemo on "20,000 Leagues Under the Sea."

Lost River Delta: Travel to the Lost River Delta to experience an adventure in the vein of "Indiana Jones Adventure: Temple of the Crystal Skull." Adventurers must see this exhilarating attraction.

Arabian Coast: Experience the magical realm of Aladdin and Sinbad while exploring the Arabian Coast. Don't miss the captivating "The Magic Lamp Theater" show.

Mysterious Island: Mysterious Island, nestled within the shadow of the mighty Mount Prometheus, is home to thrilling rides like "Journey to the Center of the Earth" and "20,000 Leagues Under the Sea."

Mermaid Lagoon: Dive into the whimsical world of "The Little Mermaid" at Mermaid Lagoon. This underwater paradise is perfect for family-friendly attractions and interactive experiences.

Port Discovery: Aquatopia and StormRider are just a couple of the futuristic activities available at Port Discovery. It's an exciting look into what the future might hold.

Magical Memories Await

DisneySea and Tokyo Disneyland are destinations where unforgettable experiences are made. These theme parks provide an unparalleled escape into the Disney universe, whether you choose to wander the charming streets of Tokyo Disneyland or take part in exhilarating adventures in DisneySea. Tokyo Disney Resort is a location where magic comes to life and dreams take flight because to its endearing characters, fascinating shows, and exhilarating rides. Come join the wonder at Tokyo Disneyland and DisneySea and share in the enchantment. I can promise you that you will always treasure this journey.

SENSO-JI TEMPLE AND ASAKUSA CULTURE

Senso-ji Temple and Asakusa Culture: Unveiling Tokyo's Rich Heritage

In the heart of Asakusa, Tokyo's historic district, stands a treasure trove of culture and spirituality: Senso-ji Temple. This ancient temple, Japan's oldest, is a beacon of tradition, offering visitors a profound journey through time and a glimpse into Tokyo's storied past.

Senso-ji Temple: A Timeless Marvel

Your attention is instantly drawn to the enormous Kaminarimon Thunder Gate as you get closer to Senso-ji Temple because it is equipped with a massive crimson lantern. All visitors who want to tour the temple grounds are greeted at this majestic gateway. Nakamise-dori, a busy street surrounded by booths selling a variety of traditional souvenirs, food, and crafts, is found after passing past the gate. It's a sensory experience that transports you to Japan's bygone era.

The Hondo, the temple's main hall, is a work of exquisite architecture. You'll be welcomed inside by a calming atmosphere, the aroma of incense, and the warm glow of flickering candles. Visitors can make wishes and give prayers here while also feeling the deep spiritual connection that has lured pilgrims for generations.

Asakusa Culture: Embracing Tradition

The cultural diversity of Asakusa stretches beyond Senso-ji Temple and into its very streets. Visitors can see a live tapestry of tradition and modernity in the area, which preserves the essence of ancient Tokyo.

Asakusa Culture and Tourist Information Center: Ascend to the Asakusa Culture and Tourist Information Center for a breathtaking vista of Tokyo. From its viewing deck, you can take in Tokyo's strikingly contemporary skyline and distant attractions like the Tokyo Skytree. It's a vivid illustration of Asakusa's unique blend of old and new.

Traditional Festivals: Japanese festivals are synonymous with Asakusa. Awe-inspiring fireworks are displayed each year during the Sumida River Fireworks Festival (Sumidagawa Hanabi Taikai), drawing tourists from all over the world. Additionally, you may take in boisterous processions, traditional music, and mesmerizing dance performances during the Sanja Matsuri, one of Tokyo's biggest and liveliest festivals.

Asakusa Rox Shopping Complex: For a modern shopping experience, explore Asakusa Rox, a contemporary shopping complex just steps away from Senso-ji Temple. Here, you can indulge in fashion, accessories, and eclectic dining options, all while enjoying a view of the bustling streets below.

Cultural Workshops: To interact with conventional Japanese arts and crafts, visit Asakusa. Take part in tea ceremonies, calligraphy classes, or even try your hand at making a ningyo, a type of traditional Japanese doll. These encounters give a stronger link to Japan's cultural foundations.

Asakusa: Where Past and Present Merge

Asakusa is a district where traditional practices and modern lifestyles live peacefully, serving as a living example of Tokyo's enduring appeal. It's a location where the architectural tranquility of Senso-ji Temple meets the contemporary energy of Tokyo Skytree. Asakusa welcomes you with open arms and invites you to cross the bridge between tradition and modernity, whether you're looking for a taste of Japanese history, a look at its contemporary innovations, or a blend of both. Discover the neighborhood's streets, ingratiate yourself with the locals, and see Asakusa's rich history come to life. Welcome to Asakusa, where age-old customs are still practiced and every opportunity exists to experience Tokyo's rich cultural heritage.

TSUKIJI FISH MARKET AND CULINARY DELIGHTS

In the bustling heart of Tokyo, Tsukiji Fish Market stands as a testament to Japan's love affair with seafood. This vibrant market, steeped in tradition, is a sensory wonderland where the freshest catches of the day converge, and culinary delights await those who venture into its lively alleys.

Tsukiji Fish Market: A Seafood Extravaganza

Tsukiji Fish Market, often referred to as the "Kitchen of Tokyo," is the largest wholesale fish and seafood market in the world. Its origins date back to the early 20th century, making it an integral part of Tokyo's cultural and culinary heritage.

Outer Market: Tsukiji's outer market is a hive of activity where guests can explore a colorful array of stalls and shops.

There is a ton of fresh seafood available here, from delicious sushi and sashimi to grilled fish and seafood skewers. You are enticed to indulge in scrumptious treats by the alluring aroma of street cuisine that permeates the air.

Inner Market: Although the core wholesale market has moved to Toyosu, seafood lovers still adore visiting Tsukiji's outside market. Stroll through narrow lanes lined with stalls offering a diverse selection of marine treasures, including uni (sea urchin), maguro (tuna), and ebi (shrimp).

Sushi Breakfast: Unmissable on any trip to Tsukiji Fish Market is a classic sushi breakfast. This early-morning treat is provided by many restaurants in the area, allowing you to enjoy the finest sushi and sashimi made from the freshest seafood.

Culinary Exploration Beyond Seafood: Beyond fish, Tsukiji offers a variety of other foods. Fans of Japanese street food will find the market to be a veritable gold mine. Every taste is catered to by the market's wide culinary scene, which includes mouthwatering tempura, savory yakitori, and sweet taiyaki.

Tsukiji: A Culinary Adventure

The Tsukiji Fish Market offers a unique culinary experience in addition to being a place to buy seafood. Here, you may interact with local sellers, enjoy tastings that emphasize the delectable flavors of Japan's marine wealth, and watch experienced chefs expertly prepare meals.

Beyond the Market: The gastronomic marvels of Tsukiji go beyond the confines of the market. The surrounding Tsukishima district is famed for its okonomiyaki, a savory Japanese pancake, and monjayaki, a savory pancake stuffed with a variety of toppings. These dishes represent Tokyo's diversified culinary scene and provide a wonderful change from seafood.

Tsukiji: A Seafood Haven

Tsukiji Fish Market invites you to explore the depths of Tokyo's culinary culture, where seafood reigns supreme, and every meal is a celebration of freshness and flavor. Tsukiji offers a seafood paradise that tantalizes the senses and leaves an imprint on your trip to Tokyo, whether you're enjoying sushi for breakfast, tasting street food delights, or exploring nearby districts for uncommon culinary experiences. Welcome to Tsukiji Fish Market, where every meal is a gastronomic joy and every taste is a tribute to Japan's oceanic treasures.

KOISHIKAWA KORAKUEN: A Timeless Oasis

Nestled in the heart of Tokyo lies Koishikawa Korakuen, a cherished gem among the city's historic gardens. With its roots tracing back to the Edo Period (1600-1867), this exquisite landscaped garden beckons visitors to embark on a serene journey through nature's beauty.

A Tapestry of Natural Wonders: A living example of Japanese garden design creativity is Koishikawa Korakuen. Its winding paths take you past meandering streams, calm ponds, lush groves, and fascinating rock formations. Every step is a revelation due to the harmonic coexistence of meticulously managed landscapes and unspoiled natural beauty.

Seasonal Splendor: Even though Koishikawa Korakuen charms visitors all year round, it truly shines in the spring's vivid hues and the autumn's flaming brilliance. For those who enjoy hanami (flower gazing), cherry blossoms cover the garden in exquisite petals in the spring, transforming it into an enchanting environment. The garden is transformed into a captivating tapestry of reds and golds in the autumn by the blazing leaves. These times of year provide an unrivaled chance to immerse yourself in nature's ever-evolving magnificence.

A Sanctuary of Tranquility: Koishikawa Korakuen is a quiet haven of peace within the vivid urban tapestry of Tokyo. It's a location where the city's beat becomes a soft whisper, letting you escape the commotion and savor some time alone for contemplation. You can take a break from the rigors of contemporary life here and rediscover the simple joys of nature.

Koishikawa Korakuen: A Timeless Treasure

In addition to being a garden, Koishikawa Korakuen serves as a living example of Japan's rich cultural legacy and a gateway to the spirit of nature. A new chapter in the garden's history is revealed with each passing season in this spot where the past and present meet. Koishikawa Korakuen invites you to discover its everlasting charm whether you're looking for the vivid hues of spring, the fiery tapestry of fall, or the serene beauty of nature. Welcome to Koishikawa Korakuen, where each visit is a trip into the heart of Tokyo's living legacy and where the music of nature coexist with the whispers of history.

TEAMLAB PLANETS: An Immersive Digital Wonderland

Located in the vibrant district of Odaiba, teamLab Planets is a captivating multimedia exhibit that invites visitors into an enchanting world of digital artistry. While its predecessor, Borderless, has closed its doors, teamLab Planets continues to dazzle with its innovative and interactive displays, spanning an expansive 100,000 square meters.

Similar to Borderless, teamLab Planets takes you on a sensory trip through a network of connected rooms, each of which is decorated with captivating digital pieces of art that come to life in front of your eyes. But what makes Planets stand out is its singular element—an installation that invites viewers to submerge themselves in knee-deep water, producing an unmatched mix of reality and art.

You'll be immersed in a symphony of colors, light, and sound as you explore teamLab Planets' immersive exhibits, transcending the limitations of conventional art. It's a sensory and imaginative experience that turns each step into a thrilling study of the virtually endless possibilities of digital creativity.

Tickets for teamLab Planets are easily accessible on Klook for anyone looking to engage on this incredible journey. This gives you the chance to take part in a creative adventure that blurs the boundaries between the virtual and real worlds. Welcome to teamLab Planets, a place where creativity has no bounds and every moment is a work of immersive art.

CHAPTER 6
DINING AND CUISINE

SUSHI AND SASHIMI

When in Tokyo, you simply cannot miss the opportunity to indulge in the culinary wonders of sushi and sashimi, two iconic Japanese dishes that epitomize precision, freshness, and exquisite taste.

Sushi: A Work of Art

Sushi, often considered Japan's culinary masterpiece, is a delightful marriage of vinegared rice, fresh seafood, and an array of ingredients. Here are some key points to savor sushi to the fullest:

Types of Sushi:

Nigiri Sushi: These are little, hand-pressed pieces of rice with a fresh fish or seafood slice on top. It's a conventional sushi dining experience.

Sashimi: While not technically sushi, sashimi consists of thinly sliced raw fish or seafood. It showcases the pure essence of the ingredients.

Wasabi and Soy Sauce: When enjoying sushi, use wasabi sparingly, as it's already added to the sushi by the chef. Dip your sushi lightly into soy sauce fish-side down to savor the flavors without overwhelming them.

Sashimi: The Essence of Freshness

Sashimi celebrates the purity of fresh seafood in its most unadulterated form. Here's how to savor this delicacy:

Varieties of Sashimi: Explore a wide array of sashimi, including maguro (tuna), sake (salmon), hamachi (yellowtail), and more. Each offers a unique taste and texture.

Condiments: The usual condiments for sashimi include soy sauce and wasabi, allowing you to adjust the spice to your taste. Remember that a little goes a long way.

Etiquette: Chopsticks should be used with care when handling sashimi, and each mouthful should be taken carefully to appreciate the subtleties of flavor and texture.

Sushi and Sashimi Dining Tips:

Freshness is Key: Seek out reputable sushi or sashimi restaurants known for sourcing the freshest ingredients. Many places in Tokyo boast daily deliveries from Tsukiji Fish Market, ensuring top-notch quality.

Omakase: A customised sushi or sashimi experience created by the chef for you is called an omakase dinner, which you might want to try. Guests will get the chance to sample fresh and chef-selected treats.

Local Recommendations: Obtain restaurant recommendations from the community or other tourists. They frequently have useful knowledge of local favorites and hidden gems.

Try Different Varieties: Don't restrict yourself to a single fish or seafood kind. Try new things and enjoy the many different flavors that Tokyo has to offer.

Respect the Chef: It's usual to say "Itadakimasu" to the chef at the sushi counter before beginning your meal and "Gochisousama" to say "thank you" when you're done.

Tokyo is a sushi and sashimi lover's dream, with everything from inexpensive street vendors to Michelin-starred restaurants. The enjoyment of these Japanese specialties is a crucial component of your culinary tour of Tokyo, whether you choose a relaxed encounter at a neighborhood sushi joint or a formal dinner occasion. So go on a culinary excursion, enjoy the artistry of sushi and sashimi, and lose yourself in Tokyo's delights.

RAMEN, TEMPURA, AND OTHER JAPANESE DELICACIES

Tokyo's culinary landscape is a rich tapestry of flavors, and when it comes to Japanese cuisine, you're in for a delightful adventure. Let's explore some of Tokyo's most beloved delicacies, including ramen, tempura, and other culinary treasures.

1. Ramen: A Bowl of Comfort

Ramen is more than just a noodle soup; it's a comforting and soul-warming experience. Tokyo offers various regional styles, but here's a glimpse of what to expect:

Tonkotsu Ramen: Indulge in a creamy, pork-based broth with thin noodles and tender slices of chashu (braised pork belly).

Shoyu Ramen: This ramen has a delicate soy sauce flavor and is frequently served with garnishes like green onions and bamboo shoots.

Miso Ramen: The showpiece of this dish is a substantial, thick broth made from fermented soybean paste (miso), which is generally served with corn and butter for a unique twist.

Tsukemen: This particular method allows you to dip and relish each bite in a rich, concentrated sauce because the noodles are served separately from the sauce.

2. Tempura: Crispy Perfection

Tempura is a culinary art form in Tokyo, showcasing the mastery of frying delicate ingredients to crispy perfection. Key points to enjoy tempura:

Variety: Discover a variety of tempura, including seasonal treats like shiitake mushrooms as well as exquisite shrimp and soft vegetables.

Dipping Sauce: Tentsuyu, a dipping sauce comprised of soy sauce, mirin, and dashi, adds a flavorful kick to each piece of tempura.

Texture: Appreciate the contrasting textures of the crispy batter and the tender, perfectly cooked ingredients.

3. Sushi: Beyond Nigiri

While we mentioned sushi earlier, there's much more to explore in Tokyo's sushi scene. Venture beyond nigiri and sashimi:

Sushi Rolls (Maki): Take a look at some of the speciality rolls, such the hot tuna roll or the rainbow roll, which blends different types of fish and veggies.

Aburi Sushi: Enjoy the excitement of sushi that has been partially seared by the chef, who uses an open flame to improve flavor.

Sushi Train (Kaiten-zushi): Visit a sushi restaurant with a conveyor belt where you may choose your favorites as they pass by for a fun and affordable experience.

4. Okonomiyaki: A Savory Delight

Okonomiyaki is often described as a Japanese pancake or savory crepe. This meal can be customized by adding cheese, shellfish, or other things to a batter made of flour, eggs, and shredded cabbage. The okonomiyaki sauce, mayonnaise, and bonito flakes on top make for a delicious medley of flavors and textures.

5. Yakitori: Skewered Perfection

Yakitori is a quintessential Tokyo street food that features skewered and grilled chicken (or other meats) seasoned with salt or savory sauces. If you want an authentic experience, head to Yakitori alleys like Omoide Yokocho in Shinjuku.

6. Gyoza: Dumpling Delights

Gyoza are pan-fried or steamed dumplings filled with a mixture of ground meat and vegetables. They're often served with a dipping sauce and can be found at local eateries and izakayas (Japanese pubs).

7. Wagyu Beef: A Culinary Indulgence

Tokyo is a meat lover's heaven where you can enjoy the world-famous Wagyu beef in a variety of dishes such tender steaks, shabu-shabu, and yakiniku grilling.

IZAKAYAS AND JAPANESE DINING ETIQUETTE

When in Tokyo, one of the most authentic and enjoyable ways to experience Japanese cuisine and culture is by visiting izakayas, traditional Japanese pubs. These cozy establishments offer an array of small dishes, alcoholic beverages, and a convivial atmosphere. Here's a guide to navigating izakayas and observing Japanese dining etiquette:

1. Understanding Izakayas:

Casual Dining: Izakayas are informal restaurants where locals congregate to unwind after work or on the weekends.

Diverse Menu: A variety Japanese foods are available, including tempura, sashimi, grilled skewers (yakitori), grilled skewers (okonomiyaki), and sashimi.

Drink Selection: Izakayas offer an extensive selection of alcoholic beverages, including sake, shochu, beer, and various cocktails.

2. Ordering and Sharing:

Small Plates: Izakaya dishes are typically served in small, shareable portions. This allows you to try a variety of flavors during your visit.

Point and Order: You should not be afraid to point to things on the menu or, if possible, present food models because some izakayas might not have English menus.

3. Drinking Etiquette:

Kanpai (Cheers): Make eye contact and say "Kanpai!" when toasting with friends or other customers. It is a happy and traditional way to celebrate.

Pour for Others: Pouring beverages for others is considered nice, especially when you see their glass is empty. They might return the favor.

4. Dining Etiquette:

Use Chopsticks: Use the chopsticks if they are offered to pick up and eat your food. Do not stick them upright in a bowl of rice, as it resembles a funeral ritual.

Sharing Is Caring: Make sure to offer the food to others before taking any that you order for the table. Dining in Japan typically involves sharing.

Slurping Noodles: Slurping while eating noodles, especially ramen, is allowed and even encouraged. It is a sign that the lunch was enjoyable.

5. Paying the Bill:

Tsumami: Some izakayas charge a seating fee known as "tsumami," which includes a small appetizer. Confirm whether this fee applies before ordering.

Cash Preferred: Although some izakayas accept credit cards, it's best to have cash because many smaller businesses prefer it.

6. Dining Responsibly:

Moderation: Be careful when drinking, especially in social settings like izakayas. Overindulgence is typically discouraged.

Designated Drivers: To protect everyone's safety if you're with a group, think about appointing a designated driver or taking the bus or train.

7. Respect the Atmosphere:

Quiet Enjoyment: Izakayas are places to unwind and have fun. To make sure that all customers are in a comfortable environment, keep noise levels down.

Engage with Locals: If you're open to socializing, strike up a conversation with locals. It can lead to memorable cultural exchanges.

A trip to an izakaya gives you the chance to become immersed in Japanese social conventions and traditions in addition to enjoying wonderful food and drinks. You'll develop connections that go beyond the plate if you follow proper dining etiquette and interact politely with locals. So, raise your glass, say "Kanpai," and relish the authentic izakaya experience in Tokyo.

CHAPTER 7
SHOPPING IN TOKYO

AKIHABARA: ELECTRONICS AND ANIME

When it comes to Tokyo's vibrant neighborhoods, Akihabara stands out as an electric wonderland where technology, pop culture, and gaming converge. Known affectionately as "Akiba" by locals, this district is a must-visit for anyone interested in electronics, anime, manga, and gaming. Here's a guide to navigating the neon-lit streets of Akihabara:

1. Electronics Haven:

Gadget Galore: The term "akihabara" is often used to describe modern electronics. You can find anything you're looking for here, including the most recent smartphones, high-end cameras, and rare electronic parts.

Duty-Free Shopping: Tourists can enjoy tax-free discounts on a variety of things by buying at one of the many Akihabara establishments that offer duty-free shopping. Remember to bring your passport along for identification.

2. Anime and Manga Paradise:

Otaku Central: The heart of otaku culture is Akihabara. Explore multi-story anime stores that are stuffed with manga, action figures, character merchandise, and collectibles. Animate and Mandarake are two well-known destinations for enthusiasts.

Maid Cafes: Discover the fascinating phenomenon of maid cafés, where waiters in maid costumes offer a fun dining experience. It is the ideal combination of food and entertainment for the curious tourist.

3. Gaming Galore:

Video Game Arcades: Akihabara is home to sprawling video game arcades, such as SEGA and TAITO Station. Test your skills on classic and modern games, from rhythm games to claw machines.

Retro Gaming: Collectors and anyone looking for nostalgia can find retro games in Akihabara stores. You can find vintage consoles, cartridges, and accessories.

4. Electric Atmosphere:

Neon Wonderland: At night, the district's streets are alive with neon billboards and signs. It's a fantastical and intriguing scene that should be seen after sunset.

Cosplay Sightings: Be prepared to see cosplayers dressed as their preferred anime or video game characters. It's a typical occurrence and evidence of the district's thriving culture.

5. Maid Cafe Experience:

Unique Dining: Known for its maid cafés, Akihabara offers a fun and engaging dining experience with waitresses dressed as maids. Travelers find the combination of meals and entertainment to be appealing.

Reservations Recommended: Maid cafes can be popular, so consider making a reservation, especially during peak hours.

6. Explore with an Open Mind:

Language Barrier: Although some establishments offer English signage and workers, it can be beneficial to have some basic Japanese words on hand to make your shopping trip go more smoothly.

Cash Is King: Although some restaurants and larger retailers might accept credit cards, it's best to bring cash because many smaller retailers only accept cash.

7. Stay Informed:

Events and Specials: Watch out for specialized occasions, campaigns, and savings. Because Akihabara is so vibrant, there is always something exciting going on.

A sensory extravaganza, Akihabara provides a window into Tokyo's modern and underground worlds. Whether you're an anime fan, an electronics enthusiast, or just an inquisitive traveler, Akihabara's unique offerings and lively environment will captivate you. Immerse yourself in the worlds of technology and pop culture, and let the neon lights of Akihabara serve as a map for your journey of Tokyo.

HARAJUKU: FASHION AND STREETWEAR

Harajuku is Tokyo's fashion mecca, a district where creativity knows no bounds. Renowned for its trendsetting streetwear, unique boutiques, and eclectic fashion scenes, Harajuku is a must-visit for anyone with an interest in style and self-expression. Here's a glimpse into the colorful world of Harajuku:

1. Takeshita Street: The Epicenter of Harajuku Style:

Fashion Wonderland: The center of Harajuku's fashion scene is Takeshita Street. It's a little, pedestrian-only street lined with lovely boutiques, vintage shops, and clothing stores.

Cosplay and Youth Culture: Japan's young culture is centered around Takeshita Street, where you can purchase a wide variety of clothing, from gothic and cosplay outfits to Lolita fashion.

2. Kawaii Culture:

Kawaii Fashion: Harajuku is synonymous with kawaii, the Japanese concept of cuteness. Explore shops like 6%DOKIDOKI and listen flavor for a dose of playful and whimsical fashion.

Harajuku Girls: You can come across Harajuku boys and girls who wear kawaii-inspired clothing, accessories, and makeup.

3. High-End Shopping:

Omotesando Avenue: Takeshita Street is a short distance away from Omotesando Avenue, well known as Tokyo's Champs-Élysées. Here you will find luxury shops, upscale clothing companies, and stunning buildings.

4. Vintage Treasures:

Harajuku Vintage Shops: Shops in Chicago and Santa Monica are great places to explore the world of vintage clothing. Find one-of-a-kind items from bygone eras, and develop your own distinctive look.

5. Trendsetting Boutiques:

Hidden Gems: Harajuku is dotted with hidden boutiques that cater to niche fashion tastes. Visit Cat Street and Laforet Harajuku for a mix of well-known brands and up-and-coming fashion designers.

Unique Finds: Whether you're into alternative fashion, streetwear, or avant-garde styles, Harajuku has something for everyone.

6. Street Food and Sweets:

Treats and Eats: Enjoy delicious street cuisine and desserts after a shopping binge. Try rainbow cotton candy, colorful crepes, and other treats.

7. Cosplay Culture:

Cosplay Stores: If you enjoy cosplay, look for specialty shops that sell costumes, wigs, and other accessories so you may dress up as your favorite characters.

Meiji Shrine Park: Cosplayers frequently congregate in Meiji Shrine Park, next to Harajuku, to display their outfits, especially on the weekends.

8. Fashion Events:

Fashion Shows: Watch out for fashion-related events and performances, which frequently occur in Harajuku. It's an opportunity to see up-and-coming designers and original collections.

9. Respect the Fashion Culture:

Ask for Permission: If you want to snap pictures of people wearing interesting clothing, you need first get their permission. It is crucial to respect consent and personal space.

Fashion can be used as a means of self-expression in Harajuku. Whether you're an avid fashionista or simply curious about Tokyo's fashion subcultures, a visit to Harajuku promises an immersive and unforgettable experience. It is a neighborhood that honors variety, uniqueness, and the limitless creativity that characterizes Japanese street fashion. So dress in your most fashionable outfit and enter the energetic Harajuku.

TRADITIONAL CRAFTS AND SOUVENIRS

While Tokyo is renowned for its modernity and bustling urban life, it's also a city deeply rooted in tradition and craftsmanship. When it comes to finding exquisite souvenirs and authentic Japanese artistry, Tokyo offers a treasure trove of options. Here's a guide to discovering traditional crafts and souvenirs in this dynamic metropolis:

1. Asakusa Nakamise Shopping Street:

Ancient Tradition: Nakamise is one of Tokyo's oldest shopping streets, and it is situated close to Senso-ji Temple in Asakusa. Along its length are shops offering traditional Japanese wares including hand-painted masks, yukata (summer kimonos), and folding fans.

Senbei Sampling: Don't miss the opportunity to taste senbei (rice crackers) offered in various flavors. They make for delicious, portable souvenirs.

2. Edo Kiriko Glassware:

Artistic Glass: Edo Kiriko is a traditional glass-cutting technique from the Edo period (17th to 19th century). Craftsmen create intricate patterns on glassware, such as cups, vases, and plates. You can find these elegant pieces at select shops in Tokyo.

3. Yosegi Zaiku:

Intricate Woodwork: Yosegi Zaiku is a traditional Hakone woodworking craft. Using small, contrasting pieces of wood, artisans assemble complex designs. Look for items with these captivating patterns on coasters, trays, and puzzle boxes.

4. Origami Art:

Paper Magic: Paper folding is a treasured Japanese tradition known as origami. You may buy origami paper and instructional guides to make your own delicate paper designs, such as cranes and cherry blossoms.

5. Japanese Calligraphy Supplies:

Brush and Ink: You may find brushes, ink sticks, and washi paper at art supply stores if you're fascinated with Japanese calligraphy (shodo). Additionally, you may get calligraphy packages that include the necessary supplies for learning this age-old craft.

6. Furoshiki:

Versatile Wrapping Cloths: Furoshiki are square pieces of cloth used for wrapping and carrying various items. They come in a range of patterns and sizes and can be both functional and decorative.

7. Traditional Sweets:

Wagashi Delights: Try some wagashi, the traditional Japanese sweets. These lovely gifts are exquisite confections that frequently depict the changing patterns of the seasons.

8. Noren Curtains:

Functional Art: Noren curtains are window or doorway-hung decorative fabric partitions. They are a useful and beautiful addition to your house because they are available in a variety of styles and sizes.

9. Antique Markets:

Noren curtains are decorative fabric partitions that are hung in windows or doorways. They are a useful and beautiful addition to your house because they are available in a variety of styles and sizes.

Treasure Hunt: Tokyo hosts various antique markets, like the Oedo Antique Market at Tokyo International Forum.

These markets offer a wide array of vintage items, from ceramics to textiles.

10. Artisan Workshops:

Hands-On Experience: Consider participating in traditional craft workshops where you can create your own pottery, ceramics, or textiles under the guidance of skilled artisans. It's a unique way to learn and bring home a personalized souvenir.

11. Aki-Oka Artisan Shops:

Hidden Gems: Visit the Aki-Oka artisan stores that are close to Okachimachi and Akihabara. These specialty shops sell handcrafted goods and one-of-a-kind items that exemplify Japanese craftsmanship.

12. Tokyo Station Character Street:

Kawaii Collectibles: Tokyo Station's Character Street is a haven for fans of Japan's cute and quirky pop culture characters. You can find character-themed merchandise, toys, and stationery.

Traditional crafts and trinkets from Tokyo make lovely souvenirs of your trip and serve as a reminder of Japan's long tradition of fine craftsmanship and artistic achievement. You'll find the ideal souvenirs to bring back from Tokyo's markets, streets, and boutiques, each of which tells a tale of the country's rich cultural tapestry. Therefore, immerse yourself in the realm of traditional Japanese handicraft and leave Tokyo with treasured souvenirs that embody this extraordinary city.

CHAPTER 8

TOKYO'S NIGHTLIFE

KARAOKE AND ENTERTAINMENT

As the sun sets over Tokyo, the city undergoes a mesmerizing transformation into a bustling hub of nightlife and entertainment. Among the myriad options available for a memorable evening, karaoke holds a special place in the hearts of both locals and visitors alike. Here's your comprehensive guide to experiencing the best of Tokyo's karaoke and entertainment scene.

Karaoke Culture in Tokyo

In Japan, karaoke is more than just singing; it is a deeply embedded cultural phenomenon. Tokyo has an astounding selection of karaoke establishments. These places range from cozy bars where you can sing for a small group of friends to multi-story karaoke centers that provide an all-around entertainment experience.

Private Karaoke Rooms

The accessibility of private rooms is one of the distinctive aspects of Tokyo's karaoke scene. You and your friends can sing your hearts out in these spaces without worrying about performing in front of an audience. Private karaoke rooms offer the perfect environment to bring out your inner star, regardless of how experienced you are as a singer.

Song Selection for Every Taste

When it comes to karaoke in Tokyo, barriers to language are nothing. To ensure that everyone can participate in the enjoyment, the majority of karaoke machines provide a wide variety of songs in different languages. There is a significant selection of songs available, whether you prefer pop, rock, J-pop, or even anime theme songs.

All-Inclusive Karaoke Packages

To enhance your karaoke experience, many venues offer all-inclusive packages that typically include unlimited singing time and drinks for a set duration. These packages make for a carefree night of entertainment, allowing you to focus solely on enjoying the music and camaraderie.

Tips for a Memorable Karaoke Night

Reservations are a smart move, especially at popular karaoke spots, as they tend to get crowded, especially on weekends. You can start your karaoke adventure right away if you arrive with a spot reserved.

The majority of karaoke establishments also include menus with a range of snacks and drinks, allowing you to refuel and maintain your energy levels throughout your singing marathon. Just keep in mind that having fun is the main objective. Sing your heart out, enjoy the laughing, and take pleasure in the camaraderie of your friends.

Beyond Karaoke: Tokyo's Entertainment Hotspots

The primary attraction of Tokyo's nightlife is karaoke, although there are many more ways to have fun than singing. The city is filled with live music pubs, jazz clubs, and underground music venues where you may see performances by national and international performers.

Tokyo's izakayas (Japanese pubs) in neighborhoods like Golden Gai and Shinjuku's Kabukicho provide a genuine flavor of the city's evening culture for those looking for a more traditional experience. These inviting places provide a variety of Japanese foods and drinks, making them the ideal place to relax and mingle.

Themed Entertainment Experiences

Unique themed entertainment establishments that promise life-changing experiences can be found in Tokyo. For instance, the Robot Restaurant in Shinjuku offers a captivating trip into a futuristic world of robots, neon lights, and spectacular shows. It's a sensory overload that will undoubtedly have a lasting impression.

Magic aficionados can discover numerous theaters and performances all across the city that feature brilliant magicians pulling off mind-blowing illusions and tricks. These shows offer a special brand of magic that makes you gasp in amazement.

Safety and Courtesy

Always put safety and courtesy first when you set out on your nightlife adventure in Tokyo. Tokyo is a fairly safe city, but it's always a good idea to drink responsibly and know your limitations. Traveling with friends and staying in well-lit places will increase your sense of security while out at night.

Karaoke is simply one aspect of Tokyo's diverse nightlife, which includes a wide range of other activities. Tokyo's nightlife options promise priceless experiences, whether you're singing along to your favorite songs in a private karaoke room, indulging in cocktails at a stylish bar, or taking part in a themed entertainment extravaganza. So embrace Tokyo's vitality after sundown and let the city's exciting nightlife keep you entertained till dawn.

NIGHTCLUBS AND BARS

Tokyo's nightlife isn't complete without exploring its vibrant nightclub and bar scene. Whether you're into dancing the night away or enjoying a more relaxed evening with cocktails, Tokyo has a wide range of venues to suit every taste. Here's a guide to some of the city's top nightclub and bar districts and what you can expect:

1. Roppongi: The International Hub

One of Tokyo's most well-known nightlife areas is Roppongi, which is renowned for its multicultural atmosphere and abundance of pubs, clubs, and lounges. You can discover places here that cater to a variety of tastes, from sophisticated cocktail bars to boisterous nightclubs. Roppongi is a great spot to meet people from all over the world because it attracts both locals and expats.

2. Shibuya: Trendsetting and Energetic

Another vibrant area for nightlife is Shibuya, which is known for its iconic pedestrian scramble. A variety of trendy pubs, live music venues, and nightclubs can be found in this vibrant region. Shibuya is a favorite among Tokyo's nightlife fans because of its youthful and vibrant vibe.

3. Shinjuku: Diverse and Lively

From the upscale bars in the Golden Gai neighborhood to the neon-lit alleyways of Kabukicho, Tokyo's red-light district, Shinjuku offers a wide variety of nightlife alternatives. Golden Gai is well known for its modest, individually themed pubs that line its winding lanes. Shinjuku has it everything, whether you're looking for a relaxing bar in Golden Gai or an adrenaline rush in Kabukicho.

4. Ginza: Upscale and Stylish

Tokyo's most popular shopping area, Ginza, is transformed into a chic nightlife zone at night. Here, you will find high-end nightclubs, jazz bars, and opulent cocktail lounges. For those seeking a more elegant and sophisticated evening out, this area is ideal.

5. Shimokitazawa: Bohemian Vibes

For a more laid-back and bohemian nightlife experience, head to Shimokitazawa. This district is known for its indie music scene, quirky bars, and intimate live music venues. It's a favorite among artists, musicians, and those seeking a relaxed, alternative atmosphere.

6. Themed Bars: A Unique Experience

Tokyo is renowned for its immersive experience-focused themed bars. You can go to locations like Shinjuku's Robot Restaurant, where robots and neon lights create a futuristic spectacle, or themed bars that are influenced by video games, movies, and anime. These venues provide a one-of-a-kind entertainment experience you won't find anywhere else.

7. Jazz and Live Music: Groove to the Beat

Jazz lovers can find a vibrant jazz culture in Tokyo at places like the iconic Blue Note Tokyo. Enjoy top-notch performances in charming surroundings, frequently with top-notch food options. For jazz festivals and live music events taking place while you are there, check the listings.

8. Nightclub Entry: Dress Code and Cover Charges

Even while some bars have a more relaxed dress code, Tokyo nightclubs generally have rigorous dress codes. To make sure you match the standards, it is important to check the club's website or get in touch with them beforehand. Some clubs may also charge a cover charge, which may change based on the night and the venue. You might be able to skip large lineups and gain entrance if you arrive early.

9. Last Train and Transportation

Remember that Tokyo's trains typically cease running about midnight, and that rates for taxis might be high. If you intend to remain out late, schedule your evening so that you can catch the last train, or think about using rideshare or designated driving services.

Tokyo's nightlife offers a rich and varied tapestry of opportunities just waiting to be discovered. Tokyo's nocturnal offers ensure an amazing evening, whether you choose to dance the night away in a packed nightclub, enjoy artisan cocktails in a stylish lounge, or immerse yourself in a themed bar's distinctive atmosphere. So embrace Tokyo's nightlife's vibrancy and make the most of your nights in this dynamic city.

NIGHTTIME VIEWS OF TOKYO

When the sun sets over Tokyo, the city undergoes a magical transformation into a mesmerizing sea of lights and colors. Witnessing Tokyo's nighttime views is an essential part of any visit to this bustling metropolis. Here are some of the best vantage points to take in the breathtaking vistas of Tokyo after dark:

1. Tokyo Skytree: Touching the Stars

One of Japan's most famous monuments, the Tokyo Skytree, is both a transmission tower and an exceptional observation deck with sweeping views of Tokyo at night. Observe the city's illuminated skyline by ascending to the Tembo Deck or Tembo Galleria, both of which are perched above the city. The Tokyo Skytree's distinctive design gives the scene an additional element of appeal.

2. Tokyo Tower: An Iconic Silhouette

Another great location to take in Tokyo's nighttime beauty is the Tokyo Tower, which was designed after the Eiffel Tower. Visit the Main Deck or the Special Observatory for unmatched views of Tokyo Tower set against the city's sparkling lights.

3. Roppongi Hills Mori Tower: Urban Elegance

The Tokyo City View observation deck is located on the Mori Tower in Roppongi Hills. It offers a classy environment to take in the city's nightlife with its trendy ambiance and floor to ceiling windows. You can see as far as Mount Fuji on clear nights.

4. Tokyo Metropolitan Government Building: A Budget-Friendly Option

For budget-conscious travelers, the Tokyo Metropolitan Government Building in Shinjuku offers free admission to its twin towers' observation decks. Enjoy stunning night views of Tokyo from 202 meters above ground, all without spending a yen.

5. Rainbow Bridge: A Multicolored Marvel

The Rainbow Bridge, connecting Tokyo to Odaiba Island, is an architectural marvel and a sight to behold at night. The bridge's vivid colors, which are exquisitely lighted after sunset, give it its name. For a memorable experience, stroll along the pedestrian walkway or take in the view from Odaiba.

6. Odaiba: Futuristic Vibes

With its neon-lit towers and buildings, Odaiba, a man-made island in Tokyo Bay, presents a futuristic nocturnal scene. Visit locations like the teamLab Borderless art exhibit for an interactive digital art experience or Palette Town's

Daikanransha Ferris Wheel for a ride with breathtaking views.

7. Sumida River Cruises: A Unique Perspective

Embark on a Sumida River cruise to see Tokyo's landmarks illuminated from the water. These cruises offer a unique perspective of the city's nighttime beauty, with many boats featuring open decks for unobstructed views.

8. Observatory Bars: Sip and Savor

A number of pubs in Tokyo provide the ideal blend of delectable beverages and breathtaking nighttime views. These places provide a unique way to experience Tokyo's skyline, whether you're sipping cocktails in a skyscraper bar or savoring sake at a traditional izakaya with a view.

9. Seasonal Illuminations: Extraordinary Events

Tokyo displays a variety of seasonal illuminations that enhance the city's allure at night depending on the season. The holiday season's winter decorations, such the Tokyo Midtown Christmas lights, infuse the city with a mystical aura.

10. Tokyo Disneyland: A Magical Evening

For a different kind of nighttime experience, Tokyo Disneyland and Tokyo DisneySea offer enchanting nighttime parades and fireworks displays that light up the sky. It's a magical way to cap off a day of adventure and entertainment.

Remember to Check Operating Hours

Check the operation hours and any special events or restrictions at your preferred vantage point before heading out to take in Tokyo at night. Also take into account the weather, as clear sky improve the experience.

The views of Tokyo at night are absolutely stunning, giving a sense of the city's dynamic and constantly changing landscape. No matter whether you favor the sleek modernity of soaring skyscrapers or the romantic allure of bridges and rivers, Tokyo's nocturnal beauty will captivate you and is a must-see during your trip there.

CHAPTER 9

DAY TRIPS FROM TOKYO

BEST DAY TRIPS

While Tokyo itself is a vibrant and captivating city, there are plenty of incredible day trips you can embark on to explore the rich cultural tapestry and natural beauty of the surrounding areas. Thanks to Tokyo's efficient railway system, these destinations are just a train ride away. Here are some must-visit day trip options:

1. Tokyo Disney Resort: Magic Beyond Tokyo

While Tokyo Disneyland and Tokyo DisneySea may bear "Tokyo" in their names, they are nestled in Urayasu city, in the neighboring Chiba prefecture, about an hour east of central Tokyo. Whether you're taking the family on vacation or just looking for a fun day out, a trip to one of the Disney resorts is sure to be magical. As the only Disney park not owned by The Walt Disney Company, Tokyo Disney Resort stands apart and gives the experience a distinctive feel. Consider the unique attraction located just here, Tokyo DisneySea.

How to Get There: Easily accessible by train or bus, with an average travel time of about 55 minutes.

2. Kawagoe: Little Edo's Timeless Charm

Kawagoe, often referred to as "Little Edo," is a picturesque castle town located in Saitama prefecture, less than an hour northwest of Tokyo. Kawagoe is a lovely visit for history fans and cuisine lovers alike because of its traditional architecture that is reminiscent of the Edo period and its impressively preserved storehouses. Take a stroll down Kurazukuri Street, where attractive stores, teahouses, and restaurants have been renovated from old structures. Make sure to visit Kashiya Yokocho, a small street lined with stores selling traditional Japanese sweets.

How to Get There: Reach Kawagoe Station by train and then take a local bus to Kurazukuri Street, with an average travel time of about 50 minutes.

3. Kamakura: The Kyoto of Eastern Japan

Nestled in Kanagawa prefecture, Kamakura is a favored day trip destination, often dubbed the "Kyoto of eastern Japan" due to its wealth of cultural treasures. Visit a variety of temples and shrines, with the Kotokuin Temple's Great Buddha of Kamakura serving as a prominent highlight. The beautiful hiking paths in Kamakura provide the perfect blend of culture and environment. No matter if you decide to do it alone or take a tour, Kamakura promises an enriching experience.

How to Get There: Conveniently accessible by train, with an average travel time of about 1 hour.

4. Lake Kawaguchiko: Fuji's Serene Reflection

Of the Fuji Five Lakes, Lake Kawaguchiko in Yamanashi Prefecture is the easiest to reach from Tokyo for a day excursion. This onsen village is the perfect place for a full day of exploration because it provides beautiful views of Mount Fuji. There are many things to do, such as taking the Mt. Fuji Panoramic Ropeway, treating yourself to a soothing onsen bath, or going to the Fuji-Q Highland amusement park.

How to Get There: Take a highway bus from Shinjuku bus terminal to Kawaguchiko station, with an average travel time of about 1 hour and 45 minutes.

5. Hakone: An Onsen Paradise

A day trip to Hakone in Kanagawa prefecture ranks among the top choices for an enriching Tokyo escape. Hakone, a popular tourist destination two hours southwest of Tokyo, is known for its onsen spas, temples, shrines, hiking trails, and art galleries. Start your day early and immerse yourself in the peace and natural splendor of this gorgeous destination to make the most of your trip.

How to Get There: Commute by train to Hakone-Yumoto station, with an average travel time of about 2 hours.

From the magic of Disney to the historical allure of Kawagoe, the cultural depth of Kamakura, the calm beauty of Lake Kawaguchiko, and the onsen paradise of Hakone, these day trips from Tokyo provide a wide variety of experiences. Each tour guarantees an unforgettable experience outside of the busy city streets. On your Tokyo day outings, explore the options and make enduring experiences.

NIKKO: TEMPLES AND NATURAL BEAUTY

Nikko, a serene and culturally rich town located in Tochigi prefecture, is celebrated for its harmonious blend of ancient temples and breathtaking natural beauty. Nestled amidst lush forests and picturesque mountains, Nikko's temples, including the UNESCO World Heritage Site Toshogu Shrine, showcase intricate architecture and historic significance.

Toshogu Shrine, which is devoted to Tokugawa Ieyasu, is a work of art with complex carvings and vivid colors. Nikko offers a variety of outdoor activities outside of the temples, from calm lakes like Lake Chuzenji to beautiful waterfalls like Kegon Falls. Nikko delivers a fascinating day trip from Tokyo, whether you're looking for spiritual introspection, historical immersion, or the beauty of nature.

KAMAKURA: HISTORY AND BEACHES

Kamakura, a coastal city in Kanagawa prefecture, offers a captivating blend of historical significance and seaside allure. Known as the "Kyoto of eastern Japan," Kamakura boasts a rich cultural heritage, with numerous temples and shrines that narrate tales of its illustrious past.

HAKONE: HOT SPRINGS AND SCENIC BEAUTY

Hakone, located southwest of Tokyo in Kanagawa prefecture, is a day-tripper's paradise offering a delightful blend of natural wonders and soothing hot springs. Renowned for its onsen (hot spring) resorts and stunning vistas of Mt. Fuji, Hakone promises an unforgettable experience.

With a variety of ryokans (traditional Japanese inns) featuring open-air baths that let tourists soak while admiring stunning mountain views, Hakone's onsen resorts offer a revitalizing vacation. For those looking for additional adventure, the Hakone Ropeway offers picturesque rides over Owakudani, a region with volcanic geysers, giving passengers a bird's-eye perspective of the surroundings.

A unique but appealing experience is to board a pirate ship replica and have a calm trip over Lake Ashinoko. A stop at Hakone Shrine, famous for its recognizable orange torii gate set against a backdrop of the lake and mountains, marks the end of the tour. Hakone offers a day trip that is full of tranquility and breathtaking scenery, whether you're relaxing in hot springs, discovering volcanic wonders, or photographing nature's splendor.

CHAPTER 10

WHERE TO SLEEP AND OTHER PRACTICAL INFORMATION

ACCOMMODATION OPTIONS

In Tokyo, a vast array of accommodation options awaits, catering to a diverse range of preferences and budgets. Whether you seek opulent luxury or a cozy boutique experience, Tokyo has something to offer.

Tokyo has many hostels and guesthouses that promise comfort and safety for tourists on a tight budget. More of these recently built hostels are starting to open, some of which have won awards for their creative designs. Additionally, women-only capsule hotels offer a secure and reasonably priced lodging option.

Mid-tier and business hotels are easily accessible for people looking for a mix between privacy and convenience. These accommodations provide basic conveniences and are perfect for tourists planning to spend the most of their time exploring Tokyo's energetic streets.

Important locations like the Tokyo Imperial Palace, Nihonbashi, Roppongi, and Asakusa are home to a concentration of luxury hotels that provide 5-star service and breathtaking views of the city or the harbor. The city's top attractions and shopping areas are easily accessible from these points.

Tokyo offers a variety of hotels that not only offer cozy accommodation but also conduct interesting social events for individuals who have a taste for artistic and design-focused housing. Furthermore, camping cabins and luxurious glamping excursions are choices if you want to have a distinctive accommodation experience outside of the city. Tokyo genuinely meets the lodging needs of each visitor.

As I explore Tokyo's diverse accommodation landscape, I've encountered a variety of options that cater to different travel preferences.

1. Luxurious Oasis at The Ritz-Carlton Tokyo

For visitors looking for unrivaled luxury, The Ritz-Carlton Tokyo, located in the busy Roppongi area, offers a magnificent refuge. The hotel has a distinguished 5-star rating and offers stunning views of the city as well as first-rate service.During my stay here, I was captivated by the panoramic vistas of Tokyo Tower and the city's skyline. My stay at the hotel was extremely unforgettable because to its Michelin-starred restaurants and tranquil spa.

Website: https://www.ritzcarlton.com/en/hotels/japan/tokyo

2. Boutique Charm at Trunk Hotel

My visit to Trunk Hotel, nestled in the trendy Shibuya district, was a delightful surprise. This boutique gem seamlessly blends contemporary design with sustainable practices. The hotel's eco-friendly initiatives, including a rooftop garden, left a lasting impression. I appreciated their commitment to local and organic ingredients at the restaurant, where I savored delectable dishes.

Website: https://trunk-hotel.com/en/

3. Cultural Immersion at Ryokan Asakusa Shigetsu

I chose Ryokan Asakusa Shigetsu, a traditional ryokan located in the famed Asakusa district, for an authentically Japanese experience. This lovely inn featured yukata robes, tatami-matted rooms, and peaceful garden views. Having the renowned Senso-ji Temple nearby allowed me to become fully absorbed in Japanese culture during my stay.

Website: https://asakusashigetsu.com/en/

4. Contemporary Comfort at Andaz Tokyo

The Toranomon Hills hotel Andaz Tokyo combines contemporary elegance with traditional Japanese design. It was fascinating to stay in a large room with floor to ceiling windows that overlooked Tokyo Bay. My favorite part of the hotel was the rooftop bar, where I enjoyed handmade cocktails while taking in the city lights.

Website: https://www.hyatt.com/en-US/hotel/japan/andaz-tokyo-toranomon-hills/tyoaz

5. Quirky Capsules at Nine Hours Asakusa

152

I stayed the night at the futuristic capsule hotel Nine Hours Asakusa in search of an unforgettable experience. Although small, the capsules offered comfort and privacy. The hotel's handy location and modern decor made it an excellent starting point for discovering Asakusa's cultural attractions.

Website: https://ninehours.co.jp/en/asakusa/

6. Luxury and Style at Andaz Tokyo Toranomon Hills

The Andaz Tokyo Toranomon Hills provides an opulent experience with a dash of modern design. On my most recent trip to Tokyo, I had the honor of staying here, and it was simply amazing. The hotel is situated in the magnificent Toranomon Hills tower, which offers stunning views of the urban landscape. Elegantly designed, the large rooms come furnished with contemporary conveniences and a Japanese aesthetic. Delicious food is served at the Andaz Tavern restaurant, and the Rooftop Bar is the ideal place to sip

153

cocktails while admiring Tokyo's famous attractions. The commitment to customized treatment at Andaz Tokyo is what sets it apart from other hotels, making sure that visitors always feel like royalty.

7. Quaint Serenity at Homeikan Traditional Japanese Inn

I had the pleasure of experiencing authentic Japanese hospitality at the charming traditional Japanese inn known as Homeikan. This ryokan offers a distinctive and tranquil ambiance since it is tucked away among quiet Japanese gardens. For a realistic feel, the rooms are outfitted with tatami mats, sliding paper doors, and futon bedding. The Kaiseki-style dinner experience, where I relished wonderful Japanese delicacies, was what stuck out throughout my visit. It's the ideal location for experiencing Japanese culture while still enjoying modern conveniences.

8. Affordable Comfort at Khaosan World Asakusa Ryokan & Hostel

For travelers on a budget, Khaosan World Asakusa Ryokan & Hostel offers a welcoming environment with affordable dormitory-style rooms. During my stay, I found the atmosphere to be vibrant and friendly, perfect for meeting fellow travelers. The hostel's location in the historic Asakusa area provides easy access to popular attractions like Senso-ji Temple and the Nakamise shopping street. It's an excellent choice for backpackers seeking budget-friendly accommodation.

Website: https://khaosan-tokyo.com/asakusa-world/en/

9. Modern Elegance at Aman Tokyo

Aman Tokyo is a refuge of contemporary sophistication and beauty. The amazing panoramic views of Tokyo and the modern style had me spellbound when I visited. The rooms are roomy and elegantly furnished, giving guests a sense of tranquility in the busy metropolis. Dining in the hotel's specialty restaurant, which offers a delicious fusion of Japanese and Western cuisines, was a highlight of my trip. For tourists looking for a chic and serene hideaway, Aman Tokyo is the pinnacle of luxury.

Website: https://www.aman.com/resorts/aman-tokyo

10. Trendy Vibes at Wired Hotel Asakusa

The modern and creative Wired Hotel Asakusa is located in the center of Asakusa. The blending of contemporary conveniences with regional art and culture throughout my stay surprised me. The vivid and modern style of the hotel captures the vivacious energy of Tokyo. The common areas are great for mingling, and the on-site café offers top-notch coffee. The Wired Hotel Asakusa is a great option for tourists who want to fully experience Tokyo's bustling environment since it offers a distinctive blend of comfort and creativity.

Website: https://wiredhotel.com/asakusa/en/

11. Business Convenience at Hotel Sunroute Plaza Shinjuku

A practical option is Hotel Sunroute Plaza Shinjuku, especially for business travelers. I valued its convenient location, which made it easy to visit Shinjuku and its thriving commercial center. After a long day of meetings or touring, the rooms' comfort and amenities offer a tranquil retreat. The hotel's proximity to the city's transportation network makes getting about the city simple. The Hotel Sunroute Plaza Shinjuku is a great choice for guests that place a high priority on efficiency and convenience.

Website: https://www.sunroute.jp/english/sps/

These are just a few of Tokyo's diverse accommodation options, each offering a distinct charm and memorable experiences. Whether you seek opulence, cultural immersion, or modern comforts, Tokyo has the perfect place to call home during your visit. All of these accommodations cater to various preferences, ensuring a memorable stay in Tokyo. You can explore their websites for more information, rates, and availability.

SAFETY AND HEALTH TIPS

safety and health are paramount when traveling to Tokyo. Here are some important tips to ensure your well-being during your visit:

1. Crime and Safety:

Tokyo is considered one of the safest major cities in the world. However, it's still essential to stay vigilant, especially in crowded areas like train stations and tourist hotspots. Petty crimes like pickpocketing can occur, so keep an eye on your belongings. Japan has strict laws, and penalties for even minor offenses can be severe. Always follow local rules and regulations.

2. Emergency Services:

The emergency numbers in Japan are 119 for fires and medical emergencies, and 110 for police. There are operators who speak English. Knowing the location of the nearest embassy or consulate is important, particularly if you are a foreign traveler. They are able to help you in an emergency.

3. Health Precautions:

In general, Japan boasts top-notch medical services. To guarantee you obtain the best care possible should you need it, carry travel insurance that includes medical expenses. Make sure your vaccinations are up-to-date before traveling. Japan normally doesn't require any particular vaccinations, but it's always a good idea to check with your doctor.

4. Water and Food Safety:

Tap water in Tokyo is safe to drink, so you can confidently refill your water bottle from public taps. Japanese cuisine is renowned for its cleanliness and quality. Enjoy street food and local delicacies without worrying about foodborne illnesses.

5. Personal Hygiene:

The importance of cleanliness and personal hygiene is highly valued by Tokyo residents. Observe regional traditions, such as taking off your shoes before entering a home or particular establishments. Carry tissues and hand sanitizer because soap and towels might not always be available in public facilities.

6. Earthquake Preparedness:

As a result of Japan's location in a seismically active area, earthquakes are conceivable. Become familiar with earthquake safety measures including "Drop, Cover, and Hold On." In Tokyo, the majority of structures are built with emergency exits and they are resistant to earthquakes.

7. Allergies and Dietary Restrictions:

If you have allergies or specific dietary restrictions, learn how to communicate your needs in Japanese. Carry allergy cards or use translation apps to convey your requirements to restaurant staff.

8. Travel Insurance:

Think about getting complete travel insurance that includes coverage for lost luggage, trip cancellations, and medical emergencies. It gives you relaxation and peace of mind when traveling.

9. Prescription Medications:

Make sure you have enough prescription medication for your vacation if you need it. In case you require a refill, have a copy of your prescription and the names of your drugs in your pocket.

10. Respect Local Customs:

Tokyo residents are polite and respectful. Return the favor by following local customs, like bowing and saying

"Arigatou gozaimasu" (thank you). Avoid public displays of affection, as they are generally considered inappropriate.

By following these safety and health tips, you'll have a smooth and enjoyable trip to Tokyo while prioritizing your well-being. Safe travels!

ESSENTIAL JAPANESE WORDS AND PHRASES FOR TOURISTS

Basic Greetings:

Hello - こんにちは (Konnichiwa)

Good morning - おはよう (Ohayou)

Good evening - こんばんは (Konbanwa)

Goodbye - さようなら (Sayonara)

Yes - はい (Hai)

No - いいえ (Iie)

Thank you - ありがとう (Arigatou)

Excuse me / Sorry - すみません (Sumimasen)

Please - お願いします (Onegaishimasu)

You're welcome - どういたしまして (Douitashimashite)

Polite Phrases:

I don't understand - わかりません (Wakarimasen)

Can you speak English? - 英語を話せますか？ (Eigo o hanasemasu ka?)

What is this? - これは何ですか？ (Kore wa nan desu ka?)

How much is this? - これはいくらですか？ (Kore wa ikura desu ka?)

Where is the restroom? - トイレはどこですか？ (Toire wa doko desu ka?)

I need help - 助けてください (Tasukete kudasai)

I'm lost - 道に迷いました (Michi ni mayoimashita)

Travel Essentials:

Hotel - ホテル (Hoteru)

Restaurant - レストラン (Resutoran)

Train station - 駅 (Eki)

Bus stop - バス停 (Basu-tei)

Taxi - タクシー (Takushii)

Airport - 空港 (Kuukou)

Ticket - チケット (Chiketto)

Passport - パスポート (Pasupooto)

Dining Out:

Menu - メニュー (Menyuu)

Water - 水 (Mizu)

Coffee - コーヒー (Koohii)

Tea - お茶 (Ocha)

Delicious - おいしい (Oishii)

Bill, please - お会計お願いします (Okaikei onegaishimasu)

Shopping:

How much is this? - これはいくらですか？ (Kore wa ikura desu ka?)

Can you give me a discount? - 割引してもらえますか？ (Waribiki shitemoraemasu ka?)

I'll take it - それをください (Sore o kudasai)

Do you accept credit cards? - クレジットカードは使えますか？ (Kurejitto kaado wa tsukaemasu ka?)

Emergencies:

Help! - 助けて！(Tasukete!)

Call the police - 警察を呼んでください (Keisatsu o yonde kudasai)

I need a doctor - 医者が必要です (Isha ga hitsuyou desu)

Numbers:

1 - 一 (Ichi)

2 - 二 (Ni)

3 - 三 (San)

4 - 四 (Shi / Yon - Note: "Shi" can also mean death, so "Yon" is used in some cases)

5 - 五 (Go)

6 - 六 (Roku)

7 - 七 (Shichi / Nana)

8 - 八 (Hachi)

9 - 九 (Kyuu / Ku)

10 - 十 (Ju)

Days of the Week:

Monday - 月曜日 (Getsuyoubi)

Tuesday - 火曜日 (Kayoubi)

Wednesday - 水曜日 (Suiyoubi)

Thursday - 木曜日 (Mokuyoubi)

Friday - 金曜日 (Kinyoubi)

Saturday - 土曜日 (Doyoubi)

Sunday - 日曜日 (Nichiyoubi)

These fundamental Japanese phrases can come in handy when you visit Tokyo. Even though English is widely spoken in tourist regions, learning a few simple Japanese words will improve your experience and show that you respect the local way of life. Have fun while you're in Tokyo!

CHAPTER 11
TOKYO 5 DAY ITINERARY

DAY 1: EXPLORE THE HEART OF TOKYO

Welcome to Tokyo! We'll start your 5-day adventure in the bustling heart of the city. Tokyo is a massive metropolis with an array of attractions, so let's kick things off with a visit to some iconic spots.

Morning:

Yoyogi Park and Meiji Jingu

Yoyogi Park, a vast green haven in the city, is a tranquil place to start the day. Explore the verdant surroundings while taking in the tranquil environment.

Meiji Jingu, a majestic Shinto temple honoring Emperor Meiji and Empress Shoken, is located inside the park. Don't miss the chance to participate in the water purifying ceremony performed at the temple's entryway. It's a distinctive cultural encounter.

Mid-Morning:

Harajuku

Enter the hip Harajuku neighborhood directly across Yoyogi Park. This thriving area is renowned for its cutting-edge style and youthful energy.

Takeshita Dori is a busy street lined with unique stores and food carts. Wander around it. Harajuku is the place to witness Tokyo's fashion-forward subcultures. Explore Laforet, a shopping center at the end of Takeshita Dori, where you'll find a curated selection of unique fashion items.

https://www.google.com/maps/d/u/0/edit?mid=1z60QUaH
Ld6Jqx6LbWRThNxnG07EsoZM&ll=35.681308891405706%2C139.74434409610595&z=14

Lunch:

Japanese Crepes

Treat yourself to some local specialty Japanese crepes while you're in Harajuku. These savory or sweet treats have a variety of flavors and frequently use fresh ingredients. Consider trying animal-shaped gelato from Eiswelt Gelato, another delightful treat in the area.

Afternoon:

Omotesando, Aoyama & Roppongi

From Harajuku, proceed your investigation by moving east along Takeshita Dori. This path will take you to

Omotesando, a chic street dotted with pricey shops and cafes.

Visit Tokyu Plaza Omotesando Harajuku for a unique photo opportunity. The ceiling of the structure is covered in fascinating geometric-shaped mirrors. Discover the highly regarded modern art products at the MoMA Design Store Omotesando. Aoyama's Nezu Museum, which houses an impressive collection of East Asian art, is worth considering.

Evening:

Roppongi Hills Sunset View

End your day with a stunning view of Tokyo from Roppongi Hills' Tokyo City View And Sky Deck. Take the elevator to the rooftop to see the metropolis painted with the sun's golden rays. Even the beautiful Mount Fuji may be visible if the weather is clear.

The Tokyo City View also offers nighttime photography opportunities, so stay a little after sunset to capture the city's illuminated beauty. Later, explore the Mori Art Museum in Roppongi Hills if you'd like to see displays of modern art.

Dinner:

To suit different interests, Roppongi Hills offers a variety of dinnertime dining options. Depending on your preferences, you can enjoy Japanese food or flavors from other countries.

That concludes your first day in Tokyo, which was full of fascinating cultural encounters, fashion discoveries, and breathtaking cityscapes. Keep in mind that each of Tokyo's neighborhoods has a special charm, and that this is only the beginning of your experience.

DAY 2: SHIBUYA AND SURROUNDING GEMS

On your second day in Tokyo, we'll dive into the vibrant Shibuya district and explore its neighboring areas, each offering a distinct flavor of the city.

Morning:

Shibuya Scramble Crossing

Visit the renowned Shibuya Scramble Crossing to start your day. It's a fascinating sight to see pedestrians crossing the street simultaneously in all directions just outside Shibuya Station. Capture the well-ordered mayhem of this famous intersection, which has appeared in movies and music videos.

Late Morning:

Shibuya Center Street and Hachiko Statue

Explore Shibuya Center Street, a lively center for dining and shopping, after experiencing the scramble. It's the ideal location to purchase trendy clothing and mementos. Pay your respects to Hachiko, the Akita dog who has earned a reputation for being incredibly devoted to his owner. The Hachiko Statue is a charming representation of faithfulness.

Lunch:

Shibuya Dining

Enjoy a variety of lunchtime dining options in Shibuya. You can choose from restaurants serving both traditional Japanese food and other cuisines.

Afternoon:

Ebisu and Nakameguro

Visit the chic neighborhood of Ebisu to continue your exploration of Tokyo, which is famed for its fine food and lively nightlife. Discover the exquisite shopping and dining center known as Ebisu Garden Place.

Stroll along the Meguro River to Nakameguro, a charming area famous for its cherry blossoms during spring. Even outside of sakura season, it's a picturesque place for a leisurely walk.

Late Afternoon:

Daikanyama and Shimokitazawa

Discover Daikanyama, a trendy district filled with boutique shops, cafes, and hidden gems. It's a hub for stylish Tokyoites seeking a unique shopping experience.

Conclude your day in Shimokitazawa, a bohemian neighborhood known for its vintage stores, live music venues, and artistic atmosphere. It's a great place to explore the local arts scene.

Dinner:

Shimokitazawa has an extensive choice of restaurants, from quaint izakayas to international cuisine. Enjoy relaxing dinner in this eclectic area.

Evening:

Entertainment Options

At night, Shibuya and its surroundings come to life. Think about going to a comedy show, seeing live music, or taking in Tokyo's exciting nightlife.

As an alternative, take a leisurely stroll through Shibuya's well-lit streets to experience the buzz of the city after dark. That concludes your second day, which included urban exploration, cultural interactions, and a glimpse of Tokyo's creative side. Each neighborhood visited today offers its own distinct charm, showcasing the city's diversity.

DAY 3: TOKYO'S HISTORIC AND MODERN BLEND

For your third day in Tokyo, we'll delve into the city's rich history, explore its modern architectural wonders, and savor some of its culinary delights.

Morning:

Sensō-ji Temple in Asakusa

Start your day with a visit to Sensō-ji, Tokyo's oldest temple, located in the historic Asakusa district. The iconic Thunder Gate (Kaminarimon) marks the entrance. Explore Nakamise Shopping Street, which is dotted with shops selling regional treats, trinkets, and crafts. Try the rice crackers senbei and the doll-shaped pastries ningyo-yaki.

Late Morning:

Tokyo Skytree

Visit Tokyo Skytree, one of the tallest structures in the world, for sweeping views of the city. Enjoy the exciting Tembo Galleria level glass floor experience. Take breathtaking pictures of the Tokyo skyline while standing on the observation decks.

Lunch:

Asakusa Dining

Enjoy a traditional lunch in Japan at one of the quaint eateries close to Asakusa. Try udon noodles, sushi, or tempura for an authentic experience of Japan.

Early Afternoon:

Sumida Aquarium

Learn more about the Sumida Aquarium in Tokyo Skytree Town. It offers an immersive underwater experience and displays a variety of aquatic creatures. Admire unique aquatic species and captivating exhibits.

Late Afternoon:

Odaiba Island

To reach Odaiba, a cutting-edge center for entertainment and commerce, cross the Rainbow Bridge. Discover the attractions in Palette Town, including VenusFort and Toyota Mega Web. Visit TeamLab Borderless or TeamLab Planets (depending on availability) for a mesmerizing digital art experience.

Dinner:

Odaiba Dining

The eating options in Odaiba range from exquisite Japanese food to flavors from around the world. Enjoy your meal while gazing out at Tokyo Bay.

Evening:

Nighttime Views

Return to Tokyo Skytree at night to see the city's glistening skyline to cap off your day. The tower is beautifully illuminated after sunset, providing a different perspective.

Optional Evening Activity:

For a deeper understanding of Japanese culture, think about going to an Asakusa tea ceremony or cultural event. Your third day in Tokyo offers a well-rounded view of this vibrant city as it combines history, modernity, and creative marvel.

DAY 4: TOKYO'S URBAN DIVERSITY AND CULINARY DELIGHTS

On the fourth day of your Tokyo journey, we'll explore diverse neighborhoods, indulge in delicious Japanese cuisine, and immerse ourselves in local culture.

Morning:

Tsukiji Fish Market

Start your day off well by going to the legendary Tsukiji Fish Market (now Toyosu Market), where you can take in the lively seafood auctions, explore the market's surroundings, and eat some delicious fresh sushi for breakfast.

Late Morning:

Ginza Shopping

Take a stroll through Chuo Dori in Ginza, one of Tokyo's most popular shopping areas. High-end shops, department stores, and flagship stores can be found here. Visit the renowned UNIQLO flagship shop, which sells fashionable items at reasonable prices.

Lunch:

Ginza Dining

Enjoy lunch at one of Ginza's elegant restaurants or cozy eateries. Options range from traditional Japanese cuisine to international flavors.

Early Afternoon:

Koishikawa Korakuen Garden

Koishikawa Korakuen, one of Tokyo's oldest landscaped gardens, invites you to explore its serene beauty. Explore beautiful walking pathways, gaze upon placid ponds, and relish peaceful moments. The garden is especially beautiful in the spring and autumn.

Late Afternoon:

teamLab Planets

Visit teamLab Planets, a 3D digital art installation close to Toyosu Market. Discover intriguing installations, such as one that requires you to wade through knee-deep water. Be mesmerized by the unique space's combination of art and technology.

Dinner:

Local Izakaya Experience

By having dinner at a nearby izakaya, you may experience the heart of Japanese nightlife. These classic pubs provide an authentic culinary experience by serving a wide variety of modest foods and beverages. Try foods like edamame and yakitori (grilled skewers) and converse with the locals.

Evening:

Karaoke Fun

Embrace Tokyo's vibrant nightlife with a visit to a karaoke bar. Sing your heart out and enjoy a memorable evening of music and laughter. Many karaoke venues offer private rooms for a more intimate experience.

Optional Evening Activity:

Discover the neon-lit streets of Tokyo and the action-packed nightlife of Shinjuku and Shibuya. Observe how the city comes to life at night. Your fourth day in Tokyo combines sightseeing with delicious food to give you a flavor of both traditional and modern Japan.

DAY 5: TOKYO'S CULTURAL HERITAGE AND HIDDEN GEMS

As your Tokyo journey enters its final day, we'll delve deeper into the city's rich cultural heritage, uncover hidden gems, and savor the moments before your departure.

Morning:

Asakusa and Senso-ji Temple

Start your day in Asakusa, an area where tradition and modernity coexist. Discover the busy shopping district of Nakamise-dori, which leads to Senso-ji Temple, the oldest and most well-known temple in Tokyo. Spend some time in the temple complex, where you can pray, buy trinkets, and be immersed in a spiritual ambiance.

Late Morning:

Asakusa Culture

View the Tokyo Skytree and Asakusa's ancient neighborhoods from the viewing deck of the Asakusa Culture and Tourist Information Center. Continue exploring the region to find hidden gems like the quaint stores on Denbouin-dori Street.

Lunch:

Unagi Dining

Relish a classic Japanese dish, unagi (grilled eel), for lunch at a local restaurant. Unagi is known for its delicate flavors and unique preparation.

Early Afternoon:

Sumida Aquarium

Admire aquatic life and themed exhibits at Sumida Aquarium in Tokyo Skytree Town. Particularly captivating are the displays of jellyfish. Spend some time exploring the Solamachi shopping complex or buying souvenirs.

Late Afternoon:

Odaiba Island

Visit the cutting-edge entertainment center in Odaiba. Visit places of interest such as Palette Town, home of the enormous Ferris wheel known as Daikanransha. Visit TeamLab Borderless, an interactive digital art museum, if you haven't already.

Dinner:

Japanese BBQ (Yakiniku)

Enjoy a meal of Japanese BBQ (yakiniku), where you may perfectly grill a range of meats and vegetables. Savor the interactive and flavorful meal at a yakiniku restaurant.

Evening:

Odaiba Seaside Park

After exploring Tokyo, take a leisurely stroll through Odaiba Seaside Park. Enjoy stunning views of Tokyo Bay, Rainbow Bridge, and the city's lit-up cityscape. Take beautiful pictures of the city's glistening beauty.

Optional Evening Activity:

If you're interested in technology and innovation, consider visiting the Miraikan (National Museum of Emerging Science and Innovation) in Odaiba.

Your final day in Tokyo combines cultural exploration, culinary indulgence, and the discovery of modern attractions. It's a fitting conclusion to an unforgettable journey through this dynamic metropolis. Safe travels, and may your memories of Tokyo be cherished!

Made in the USA
Las Vegas, NV
13 December 2023